TERENCE CONRAN'S
HOME FURNISHINGS

TERENCE CONRAN'S
HOME FURNISHINGS

CONSULTING EDITOR: JUDY BRITTAIN

Little, Brown and Company
BOSTON · TORONTO

First published in 1986 in Great Britain by Conran Octopus Limited

Conceived, designed and produced by
Conran Octopus Limited

Library of Congress Catalog Card No. 86–81670
First U.S. Edition

Printed in Italy

FOREWORD

Interior design is not the prerogative of the professional and the wealthy – anybody can furnish their home with style. Sadly, soft furnishings have a rather 'homely' image and, while these qualities are important, the design side has often been neglected. This book therefore shows the best in furnishing design and provides the information and inspiration you need to reinterpret the classics and look at the basics from a new angle.

Textiles are an enormously flexible medium and offer endless colour, textural and stylistic variations. Fabric furnishings can dominate a room, provide a soothing background or be

BY TERENCE CONRAN

the linking factor in a room full of eclectic clutter. From a simple swathe of cream muslin across the top of a window to a room luxuriantly tented with fabric, textiles offer endless possibilities.
Take a fresh look at your surroundings – you may just want to change from curtains to blinds or decide you need a whole new colour scheme. **The Soft Furnishings Book** will provide you with numerous practical ideas on how to confidently and stylishly transform your home. Don't be daunted by the scale of the project . . . the most effective soft furnishings are often the easiest to make.

INTRODUCTION

Colour choice is both important and personal, for colour is the first thing that strikes one in a room, and it immediately betrays something about the owner and the owner's tastes. Some understanding of how colours work, in isolation and together, may be helpful both in choosing schemes and in anticipating their eventual effect.

Paradoxically, it is by looking at black and white (which themselves have no pigment and are strictly speaking not really colours at all) that we gain most insight into the art of working with any colour, including the rainbow spectrum of what might be called the 'colourful' colours. Black and white are the negative and positive elements, night and day, the extremes of dark shadow and brilliant light. Used alone, they make the strongest statements, and used together they form the most pronounced contrasts.

Black is perhaps the most sophisticated colour choice, especially in a city context – it seems to look out of place in country settings. Black is difficult to use on its own, for it absorbs light and will get little help from shadow play. To compensate for this lack, choose fabrics with varied surfaces so that the gloss of hard paintwork and lacquer and the smoothness of satin and leather can act as highlights to matt wools, suedes and cottons. An all-black sitting-room is very smart: think of modern black tubular furniture with highlights coming from the leather seats, the high gloss of black picture frames (perhaps surrounding black and white photographs) and the gleam of black audio and television equipment. The walls could be covered with

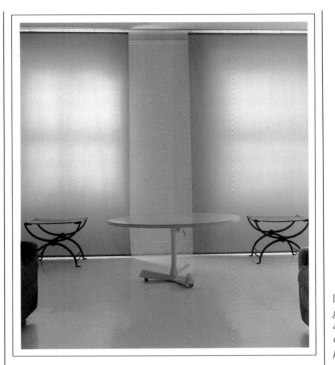

LEFT *The quality of light affects one's surroundings. Sheer curtains diffuse and soften the light that streams into this room, bathing the white walls and furnishings with a peachy glow.*

LEFT *A plain room has been given a shady feel, the restful atmosphere reminiscent of cool green woods, simply by pulling down the blinds.*

pleated black cotton, and the floors covered with nubbly black wool carpets.

Black with white looks smart and modern. Think first of white walls with black furniture. Then introduce black and white patterns: a checked tablecloth, a striped chair cover; hang etchings on the walls framed in black, and on the table place a black pot filled with Madonna lilies. Gradually the discipline will relax into an interesting experiment in the use of shapes and textures as well as of colour contrast and the impact of pattern. Finally, add a single splash of colour such as cobalt blue in the patterning of a rug.

When using black and white together, it is best to reserve a large area for one colour, so that the other becomes a focal point. Balance the proportions of the main colours with patterned elements or intermediate colours. The choice and arrangement of furniture and ornaments is vital, because, with contrasts so pronounced, all shapes will be emphasized.

White is the most popular of all paint colours, and the easiest of all colours to use.

White is clean, sparkling and fresh and needs to be kept looking that way. There is a danger of it becoming too safe and bland or looking cold and clinical. But as white reflects light, you have the potential for shadow play, so choose fabrics that fold and drape or have a distinctive texture to make maximum use of shadows as patterning and tone. In India they say there are four tones of white: the whites of the conch shell, the waves, the clouds and the moon. In fabrics, think of the creamy-white of wool, the laundry-white of linen, the pearly-grey patterning of damask and the misty clouds of gauze or lace.

True grey is the child of black and white, and its shade will vary according to which parent was dominant: think of charcoal, steel, pewter, rainclouds, newsprint (actually black dots on white, merging into tone). Grey is a

LEFT *White mixed with a strong contrasting colour always looks fresh. The lively pattern mix works because each area of pattern has a distinct weight – from the densely patterned sofa fabric to the stark lines of the rug.*

BELOW *Primary colours can look extremely sophisticated and they take on a jewel-like glow when set against black, in the same way stained glass is enhanced by a black border.*

ABOVE *The floral fabric echoes the design on the sides of the Victorian basin. Tints of sepia evoke the past besides warming the room; a fabric screen emphasizes the cosy and traditional look.*

useful main colour: picture a grey flannel sofa in any clear-coloured room. Grey is a good backdrop to clear colour, though it tends to make muted or muddy colours become dingy.

The presence of black, white and grey is flattering and enhancing to any of the primary colours. These are red for fire, blue for water and yellow for sun. Each is related to the other by marriage but not by blood, for yellow has its red side (with the meeting point making orange); it also has a blue side (they meet as green). Likewise, red has a blue side at the central point of which is violet. In each case the blue side tends to give off cold colours and the red warm ones. Clashes occur when colours are chosen from both the red and the blue sides of a colour, for instance acid green with sea green. Harmonious colours are those chosen from the same side and are near to each other on the colour wheel, for example,

RIGHT *All-white fabric offers the opportunity to experiment with subtleties of tone and texture. The blue dish and rug make splashes of colour against the pastel background and stop it looking too wishy-washy.*

green, greenish yellow and yellow. Complementary colours, those opposite each other on the wheel, retain their individual intensity when seen together.

Primaries used together benefit from being separated from one another by a frame of black or white which allows each to sing its own colour song without distortion. A plain monotone background, especially white, will

make them sing louder. Reserve a solid dark area for a calming effect on the whole.

Patterned primaries also need a solid-coloured backdrop. For example, where a room is to be predominantly red, then red walls and floor will show off the primary prints on chairs, beds and even lampshades. When duller, more muted tones of bright colours are being used together, then the whole place can be made up of a medley of pattern on pattern – as long as the colours all have something of the same weight and muted quality to them. This is especially true when rooms in old houses have been added to over the years, patterned chintzes and mellow oriental carpets accumulating alongside each other, each design made up of a family of colours that go well together. Such an atmosphere, where harmonies are more important than contrasts, can be taken up and copied today in fabrics reproduced from old designs.

Pastel colours are blues, yellows, greens

FAR LEFT *A blaze of shocking yellow felt is a suitable covering for a piece of sharp, fun furniture. The yellowness is enriched by the soft sponging on the walls. If the colour was any stronger the colour of the sofa would be diminished, a contrasting colour would make it look very strident.*

LEFT *Mellow yellow is the background for a rich harmony of warm, earthy red cushions. The picture, the exotic spicy colours, and the patterns on the textiles all contribute to the Indian theme.*

and reds paled down with white. Often subtle gradations of pastel shades are used to emphasize the architecture, with the colours being gradually increased for the silk of a cushion and again for the velvet of a chair cover. Make sure the increase is slight: a steep step will break the harmony, and a flash of really bright colour will strike a discordant note.

Combinations of many colours can thus seem bright and full of contrast, muted and richly harmonious, pale and delicate. When a room is to be in one colour only, then extra care is needed to avoid a number of pitfalls. First choose the actual colour carefully. Try it out in a corner of the room (a colour is often reinforced by its twin on the next wall) to see how it looks by day and night, under natural and artificial light. Next, vary the depth and texture of the colour – a strictly monochrome room can create an unpleasant optical illusion where the architecture begins to lose its contours through lack of definition, and the furnishing gets blurred into a smudged shape, since the surfaces are no longer defined by differences of colour and pattern. Far better to orchestrate the colour impact with deeper and paler tones of the same colouring and change texture from matt to gloss.

The shape and proportion of a room will be altered for better or worse with colour. Black will appear to diminish the size of a room; white, on the other hand, will seem to enlarge it. If the height of a ceiling or the length of a room needs to be reduced, dark colours – not necessarily black – can be chosen, and vice versa. Pale-patterned fabrics will give depth and appear to recede, while bright ones will advance and foreshorten.

Dressing rooms with colour is like painting a picture while at the same time sculpting a three-dimensional space in which to live – and how you do it is a question of personal taste. Look around for a piece of fabric whose pattern or textural qualities please *you*, analyze how that effect comes about, and use this understanding to develop a whole colour scheme from this starting point.

ABOVE *Different types of pattern can be combined if they have the linking factor of colour. If many different sizes and shapes of pattern*

*are involved they can be
grouped together into areas
of maximum activity and
separated with intervening
areas of calm.*

TEXTURE

Texture is often secondary· to the more immediate impact of colour or of striking pattern, but it is texture that adds quality to colour – the richness of deep-coloured velvet is due to its pile, the pearly gleam of silk reflects off its smooth surface, the firm even weave of cotton permits printed patterns to stand out crisply, and the softness of wool gives tweeds their muted quality.

Although we are more inclined to choose fabric because of its colour, pattern or weight, we are often already responding unconsciously to the texture of raw materials. A simple whitewashed cottage is invariably decorated in cottons and wools rather than silks and satins, which would detract from the rustic ambiance. In grand rooms, on the other hand – particularly ones that are used in the evening – rich and glowing taffetas, brocades and velvets are perfectly at home.

What is meant by texture usually describes

RIGHT *Quilting conveys a message of warmth and softness. The imposing feel of this dining-room has been subtly toned down. The soft padded surface of the quilting contrasts sharply with the brittle surface of the cane chair.*

RIGHT *The coarse weave of the tapestry blends in with the rough plastered wall and its faded shades and 'historical' feel contribute to the mellow atmosphere of the room.*

the way the light plays on the surface of a fabric. (From this we read messages, too, about the feel of the material – its potential softness, smoothness, its relative warmth or coolness.) Texture is most pronounced when the fabric's surface shows clearly a play of light and shade – through its own weave, or through some decorative treatment such as pleating or ruching. It is this patterning of light and shade that takes the place of colour contrasts in monochrome schemes and not only sustains visual interest in a plain surface but creates a positive desire to reach out and touch – it may be a button-backed sofa, a knitted cushion patterned with cables, quilting or corduroy, the herringbone weave of an upholstery fabric.

Fabric textures have their own individual feel and often evoke their own special associations. As with clothing, household fabrics have perfect partners: think of flannel with

LEFT *This room displays a combination of matt and shiny surfaces. The black velvet of the bedcover absorbs light, the shiny shell pink fabric of the curtains reflects it. Line is important in this room and the textures draw attention to it: the soft satiny knots of the curtains, the dense velvety chunk of the bed.*

BELOW *Richly coloured pile fabrics exude warmth, but their cosy image is spiced up by the golden silk curtains. In spite of its air of comfort, this is a sophisticated room.*

ABOVE *A white colour scheme is a good opportunity to make the most of texture because white reflects light. Every surface in this room has been covered in a differing soft texture: nubbly and quilted finishes, close and open weaves. A restful room that makes you want to sink back and sleep.*

starched linen, satin with velvet, tweed with linen and cotton, organdy with lace. (Think of more surprising contrasts, too – trimming a tweed-covered cushion with a border of satin, for example.) Dressing a room with such textures in mind is another way of escaping the straitjacket of colour. The way in which these fabrics are hung, draped and pleated adds extra weight to their intrinsic feel. Think of pleated linen walls and curtains, crunchy white wool rugs and a pile of quilted cushions. Think of a plain room with a blind at the window – a softly folding blind for a tailored finish, or a ruched one with frilled edges for a billowing and elaborate effect. Texture adds the third dimension to style.

RIGHT *Coarse weaves and bright folk embroidery enhance the country feel of a rustic room. A casual look has been achieved by improvising with pieces of old textile, rather than buying new furnishing fabric.*

STYLE

Style can be found in the way a bunch of flowers is organized or in the cut and hang of curtains. It doesn't have to be grand, but it is worthwhile looking at rooms put together by some of the acknowledged exponents of style. In your gut reaction to their – sometimes extreme – tastes you may find the glimmer of recognition of the way you would like to go (as well as where you would rather not). The signpost may point towards following a subtle exploration of monochrome textures, or in the direction of bold contrasts; to taking the paths of pattern, figurative or abstract; to going along with simplicity, rustic or sophisticated; or to treading among the accumulations of the confirmed collector.

Every so often some individual revolutionizes style and opens everyone's eyes to a whole new approach. The deeply coloured and patterned interiors of the Victorians were abandoned by the fashion-conscious in the Twenties when Syrie Maugham's white rooms – where everything from flowers to armchairs to statues was white – became an international craze. White is still as full of possibilities today.

The late Geoffrey Bennison comes to mind as a master of style, mixing the worn, valuable and old with the new and making the houses of the rich cosy as well as costly. He massed giant pots together on round tables covered with old embroidered cloths so they formed a landscape reminiscent of the onion domes of the Kremlin. He threw old textiles over sofas and heaped mountains of Moroccan embroidered cushions on top. Bennison never minded if a fabric was worn or frayed as long as it was beautiful. His palette was rich with tawny reds, blues, greens and gold, yet his abundance was always subdued by areas of calm. High windows were meekly dressed in plain holland blinds and floors covered in humble coconut matting. In small homes Bennison's axiom was to treat the rooms as part of a whole, using the same colour scheme throughout to produce a feeling of continuity and space.

RIGHT *A sleeping area has been constructed that harmonizes with the uncluttered lines of this apartment and makes the maximum use of space. The way the striped fabric has been stretched over the frames not only creates an extra pattern dimension, but the fabric contributes to the feeling of light and space with its cool colouring.*

26

RIGHT *The bold indigo-dyed fabrics form simple but sophisticated covers for the furniture. The room feels modern because it is uncluttered, but at the same time it is dateless.*

BELOW *Masses of white gauzy fabric and piles of pillows can look smart rather than boudoir-like. The simple white curtain, and stark lines of the table, mirror and bedside table stop this room from looking overpoweringly feminine.*

Shoe designer Manolo Blahnik's London drawing-room impressed with its simplicity, the complete antithesis to Bennison's style. The walls were hung with lengths of pale pink cotton, with the sides tied together with tapes rather than seamed. Two sofas furnished the room, one at either end, and these were covered in a deep powder-pink cotton twill. Beside one of them a huge stone head of a forgotten Greek hero rested on the floor. Strange, sparse and beautiful, but not austere.

Without the oriental carpets, giant arm-chairs and the space to display a sculpture – let alone the piece itself – how can style be created? Begin with an idea and follow it through. Think of a strong colour, double it with a second, then add a large area of white to sustain the two without conflict: perhaps emerald walls, red-covered furniture and floor, a glass-fronted cupboard hung with scarlet curtains; devote the rest of the room to glistening white paint and drifting gauze and style has crept in by way of colour.

Perhaps you would prefer pattern to do the talking. Dress the windows in a rose-patterned fabric and then use roses as a decorating theme for the rest of the room. Add pots of real garden roses and, when out of season, exchange them for dried ones.

If you are not inspired by flowers but like pattern, consider a clean-cut environment of tailored lines, close-fitting covers and orderly patterns, everything kept in its place by neatly piped edges. Furniture can be covered in plain fabrics with contrast pleating; find a wide striped fabric of the same colour with white and use it for curtains and (tightly stretched and with several coats of varnish) as a floor covering.

Build up an effective but less extreme style of room by working with tones of harmonious colours such as cream, butter yellow and tobacco brown. Cover an armchair in soft brown wool and throw a brown mohair rug over it for extra comfort. Give another chair a blond suede seat and hang folding yellow cotton blinds at the window. Collect shells, pots, jugs and other objects in interesting natural shapes and colours to put on shelves and tables. Do this in any scheme that you really love and the room will be stamped with your taste.

Collections, too, can set the theme for a room. If you have a collection of china for example, take a good look at it and see if there is a particular pattern or colour which predominates and then try to find a fabric that will echo this pattern, or copy it and stencil a border along the curtains, pelmet or cushions for a co-ordinated effect.

Study interior design magazines and work out why certain pictures catch your attention. Rather than trying to copy the patterns and effects exactly (duplication is rarely possible, since the room and the light and the constraints are always different) work out what it is about the colours and textures that appeals to you, and then echo the style in a way of your own, in the fabrics that suit your surroundings.

LEFT *An understated timeless style, the use of warm 'sun-bleached' colours and natural pale wood would make this room look sunny even on a grey day.*

Full-blown summer roses complete the picture, which illustrates a perfect combination of texture colour and style.

HISTORY

For thousands of years textiles have been used in furnishing to provide warmth, comfort, protection and decoration. They have been used as draperies, padding, hangings and coverings, to indicate status. Many of these forms of soft furnishing are with us still today: for example, divided window curtains overhung by a pelmet. Others have become redundant: the wall hanging, once necessary to keep out draughts as well as provide decoration, has virtually disappeared.

Yet the way our ancestors covered walls, doors, ceilings and chairs, and dressed beds and windows was often done with great panache. The ways in which they used fabric in their interiors, the themes and details of their styling, can be a rich source of inspiration today.

Fashions in interior design were led by a wealthy, influential minority (generally a court) and were copied by those who could afford to do so in a simpler style, according to their means.

The classical world of Greece and Rome was to influence architecture and interior decoration in the West for centuries to come. How did these early leaders of style use textiles in furnishing?

The Greeks used drapery exuberantly, either hung flat against the wall or looped and gathered in bunches, layered in different colours or draped in arches. Favourite colours were a strong green, saffron, gold, violet and crimson.

Curtains often took the place of doors in the Greek and Roman world. And as their homes were usually draughty the bed was often surrounded by curtains, sometimes richly perfumed. Couches were the most popular items of furniture, their fabric-swathed mattresses and cushions supported by straps of webbing covered with layers of drapery.

The Romans also spent much time out of doors and erected brightly coloured banqueting pavilions in gardens with canopies slung over poles.

The Importance of the Hanging

Loose drapes and hangings were also a feature of the medieval interiors of northern Europe. All the richness of these interiors was concentrated in textiles. Furniture had to be portable because of the itinerant lifestyle of the ruling classes; in order to administer his various properties, a landowner had to move from castle to castle. Bare rooms could be dramatically transformed with tapestries and embroidered hangings that could be also dyed and painted.

Different sets of tapestries were hung according to the time of year. In autumn and winter, hunting and hawking scenes were popular. Pastoral and romantic ones were associated with spring and summer. War scenes from the Crusades and the Trojan legends provided another decorative theme.

Early medieval beds had curtains that hung from the ceiling joists or from cords suspended from the walls. By the 14th century a tester, a square canopy, hung over the bed, suspended from the ceiling on rods or chains, but not yet held on posts. An early 15th-century painting of a bedroom in a French

ABOVE A rare early 18th-century English embroidery worked in linen and silk in tent stitch. One of the main functions of hangings was to exclude draughts. If there was no wainscot the gap between the hanging and the floor would be filled with worsted or coloured canvas.

During the period of Gothic architecture with its sloping ceilings, tapestry was stretched on poles just below the roof. Hangings could be moved around and used as dividers in very large rooms, creating a colourful, cosy enclave.

town house shows the bed awash with drapery, surmounted by an unusual domed tester from which cascade yards of fabric strewn with fleurs-de-lys. The drapes are matched by a wall hanging casually knotted to one side of an open door.

The Origins of Co-ordination

These matching drapes indicate an interest in aesthetics that was to develop with the Renaissance. Symmetry, regularity and harmony were principles of Renaissance architecture and fashionable interiors of the 15th and 16th centuries demanded the same harmony in their use of drapery. The fashion soon spread for all textile furnishings to match each other.

However, window curtains at this time were rarely divided to make a symmetrical pair. A thin cloth like sarsnet (a silk taffeta) or linen would have been pulled across the embrasure as a shield from the sun rather than a protection from draughts, and pelmets were not yet in evidence. Curtains did not become commonly used until late in the 17th century; by then they were divided.

Table carpets appear frequently in paintings of the 17th-century interior. Although these could be Turkey rugs that were considered too precious to be put on the floor, table carpets were not strictly carpets. This was just a generic term. They could be tapestry-woven or of richly embroidered cloth – and when they needed to be protected, they would have been covered with a linen, gauze or lace cloth.

Only very unimportant rooms in the 17th century were without wall hangings unless they were panelled. However, hangings were now made in narrow widths similar to modern wallpaper and were no longer the loosely hanging drapes of medieval times. Instead, they were fitted to the walls, and a striking effects could be achieved by alternating widths of different materials. Frequently widths of cloth would be framed by a contrasting border or the join between them disguised with a trimming of lace made from

LEFT *A reconstruction of a late medieval bath. The canopy is held taut by a hoop called a sparver. It kept the bather cosy by blocking out draughts and brought an element of privacy. The tub is lined with fine white linen which would have stopped the bather rubbing against the rough wood. The bath was emptied from a tap at the bottom and rolled away when not in use. The canopy could be lowered from the ceiling and packed away. Note the damask wall hangings suspended from rings looped over hooks.*

RIGHT *This 17th-century picture of chess players by Cornelis de Man shows several features typical of Dutch interiors at that time. The chair has a padded back and seat, but the seat back has been left uncovered. This is because chairs usually stood flanking the walls when not in use rather than being scattered around or drawn up against a table. The bed in the picture is built into the wall panelling to form a cosy box and the hangings match the 'tour de cheminée', the decorative and protective pelmet that runs along the chimney breast. This is lined with a white cloth that would have been changeable.*

silk or metal threads. The same system was used for gilt leather hangings, which came from Spain.

From the late 17th century hangings were decorated with two lengths of fringe: a longer fringe along the bottom of the hanging concealed the nails which attached the hanging to a wall batten, and a shorter one covered the vertical joins. Another neat 17th-century way with fringes was to nail them along the edges of shelves so that dust would be flicked from the top of books as they were taken out.

During this period, it was above all the upholsterer who determined how interiors would look. He had started out inauspiciously as a dealer in second-hand goods, but by the 17th century his role had not only changed but was rapidly developing as the room hangings which he supplied and fitted became more and more extensive and elaborate. Although most of the techniques of upholstery (with the exception of springing) had been mastered by the end of the 17th century largely by borrowing from saddlery, effects

RIGHT *Three textile designs that are as usable in contemporary interiors as they were during their heyday. The rich and intricate patterning of the crewel embroidery and the block print could be put to good effect in a plain room. The pretty, sprigged roller print would look attractive as either curtaining or bedcovering – or both.*

were achieved mostly with splendid materials lavishly trimmed rather than skill.

Initially the rich coverings on grand chairs were detachable; later loose covers protected upholstery which was fixed. This wrapping was supposed to be removed when the chair was in use, but 18th-century paintings show people relaxing in wooden-framed chairs dressed in rather charming baggy red-and-white-striped linen or checked loose covers, so we may asume that this quite often didn't happen.

In less exalted circles, upholstered chairs did not always match and might be covered in a motley mixture of woollen velvet, gilt leather, silk or worsted. What could almost be called an 'easy chair' with padded back, seat and arms appeared in the early 18th century in France. Caned chairs were often furnished with shaped squabs that could be tied to the back of the seat. They were like small mattresses, with the wadding secured with tufting. Great fat down-filled cushions oozed over benches and day beds.

Most rooms of any importance were furnished with window curtains by the 18th century. Divided curtains were common, but the pull-up version was considered smarter. The festoon was a single hanging that was drawn up vertically to nestle in floppy folds just below a pelmet. Others were divided and pulled up diagonally towards the upper corners of the window, to form draped festoons with drops at each side.

Throughout the 17th and into the 18th century beds were the box shape they had assumed in the 16th century, the tester being supported by the frame of the bed itself to form the classic 'four-poster'. Fashions displayed themselves in the style of the dressings with the valances that hung overhead initially straight-edged and heavily fringed, then later edged with scallops and zigzags.

As the inside of the hangings was scarcely less important than the outside, a valance was made for the interior as well, the bed curtains presumably running between the two layers.

Crewel embroidery – a detail from a 16th-century decorative furnishing cloth.

English block print, c.1780

A sprig design printed on a copper roller in Manchester, c.1820

ABOVE *This design for window curtains comes from* Ackerman's Repository, *an early 19th century catalogue, which showed the work of British designers and the latest furnishing fashions of 1809—28. This plate shows a typical Empire curtain arrangement using two weights of material: a light muslin undercurtain with a heavier overcurtain in silk. For extra prettiness, the undercurtains could sometimes be sprigged with flowers. Curtains at this time were often decorative rather than functional and, as with all Empire textile creations, relied on clever draping rather than cut or construction. They were superbly accessorized with exotic poles, bold tiebacks and pelmets and plump wobbling borders of bobbles and fringes.*

Lining material was visible on the back faces of the curtains and was normally also used for the front of the head-cloth and the counterpane or coverlet.

Materials required for furnishing and upholstering moved from one country to another. The French had the monopoly when it came to luxury goods like tapestries, furniture and carpets, but Italy provided the bulk of the silk damasks and velvets. England did not even try to compete with the French and Italians for the luxury market. Her success lay with meeting the requirements of the middle classes, both at home and in Europe, with pottery, carpets and furniture. The one frivolous English product that found popularity was, curiously enough, flock wallpaper. From the early 18th century America began to be a major consumer of European fashions, first from England and then from France.

The Triumph of the Drape

The French style that was to sweep the United States and Europe originated in the late 18th century and was called Empire because it coincided with the imperial phase of Napoleon's rule. Although Empire meant stark lines of furniture, hangings and drapes were allowed to flow in seemingly voluptuous abandon. Swathes of material were slung over curtain-poles, rooms were smothered in muslin or tented in silk. Chalky Wedgwood china colours offset by the occasional black border were among the prettier colour schemes. But the Empire style could be quite strident with satin a popular fabric, especially in shades of brilliant green, a glaring crimson and a bright yellow.

During the 18th century, beds had started to turn sideways against the walls and some had lost their posts. Testers were once more suspended from the ceiling or attached to the walls. The size of the beds was reduced and effects depended on the sweep and fall of the drapery rather than the elaborate fringes, festoons and curtains of the past. Empire beds were pretty rather than imposing.

LEFT *A modern interpretation of Empire style; the bed turns sideways to the wall and is surmounted by drapes and drooping tassels. Although the original canopy would have been loosely draped and swathed, the bedcovers would never have been so rumpled as the ones here. Beds usually had fitted covers, often heavily fringed along the edges with loops and tassels, with tightly packed bolsters at both ends.*

The double-ended wooden bed is based on an antique classical form.

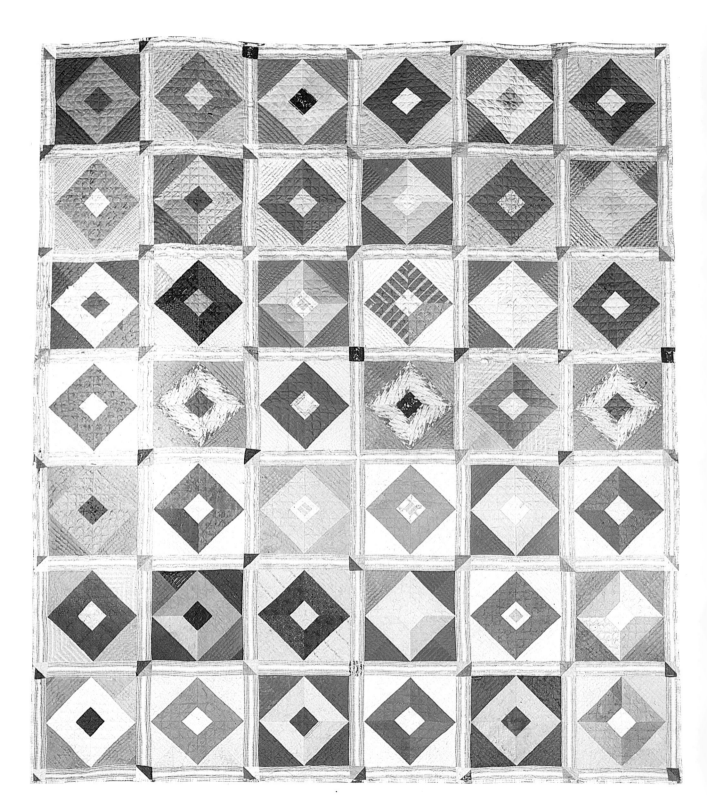

LEFT *The silks used for the top of this quilt are typical of those used in the making of Quaker dresses.*

The quilt came from the Yarnall family, who were prominent Quakers in Philadelphia. The quilt would have been made by the sewing woman employed by the family from the pieces left over from her dressmaking.

By contemporary standards, this was a luxurious quilt. It was not until the early 18th century in America that fabrics became cheap enough to cut up before they were quite worn out and the art of patchwork began to develop. Early patterns were almost always geometric and the whole family would join in cutting and assembling them.

The Age of Clutter

Drapery remained popular well into the 19th century, although wallpaper supplanted textiles as a wall covering, except in the most sumptuous houses. By the mid-19th century the chimney piece was often swathed in material. Some fireplaces even had curtains that were drawn back when the fire was lit.

The ebullient festoons and swags of material which had hitherto decorated windows gave way to the lambrequin – essentially a flat pelmet which drooped down at the sides and cut out a great deal of light. This was often used with symmetrical main curtains and with sub-curtains of muslin or lace. Roller blinds were also fitted to fashionable windows.

Springing had been developed in upholstery by the mid-19th century and deep buttoning was adopted on sofas and chairs. Up to this point tufts had been adequate as long as the upholstery stuffing remained thin, but once it grew more generous great strains were put on the securing system and only buttons proved strong enough to hold the thick chunks of wadding in place.

As the craft of upholstery grew, so did the seating, and so the familiar bulging, fit-to-burst chairs and sofas of the 19th century were born. They took pride of place in the typical dark Victorian interior which was cluttered with pouffes and footstools, cabinets, tables of knick-knacks, shawls, screens and jardinières. During the late Victorian era, the only piece of furniture that became less cluttered was the bed. The long-beloved hangings were considered unhealthy and were finally jettisoned.

Eclectic Times

Since the turn of the century there has been a general movement away from such cluttered fussy-looking interiors, sometimes to an extreme degree, and the late 20th century living-room appears very different to its 19th-century predecessor as far as density of furnishings and ornament are concerned.

LEFT *The dining-room (painted in 1898) at the Grange, a house owned by the Pre-Raphaelite painter Edward Burne-Jones. He subscribed to a reform movement in design which became known as the Arts and Crafts. In total contrast to the prevailing fussy fashions, its protagonists believed that design should be based on 'fitness for purpose' and 'truth to nature'. However, in spite of this radical streak, many of their designs were traditional and historicist, often taking inspiration from an idealized notion of medieval life. Their interiors were full of rich patterns, exotic pottery, pictures crowded with gods, monsters, knights and beautiful ladies – some of which seem to be represented on the* portière.

But, on the other hand, the informal groupings of furniture still look familiar to us and many modern sofas and chairs are very similar in design and textile covering to their 19th-century counterparts. And there is another element that we share with the second half of the 19th century – choice. By the 1850s standards of taste were being dictated by the market place rather than an aesthetic ideal based on classical values. Taste had become democratic rather than aristocratic, and mass production and mass consumption meant a multiplicity of styles. Now, as then, there is no single aesthetic standard, and we are free to dip into a rich tradition of furnishing style and reinterpret any of the looks of the past that takes our imagination.

RIGHT *The walls of this room are lined with the same damask as the curtains. Until the advent of mass-produced wallpaper, covering the walls with textiles was common in the houses of those who could afford to do so. Capping, a decorative device that first appeared in the late 17th century, runs around the room and across the window to form a pelmet. The pleated silk undercurtains were made by Fortuny.*

WALLS, DOORS
AND
CEILINGS

A room of fabric, with walls, doors and ceilings hidden behind a covering of cloth, makes an entirely new space. It becomes a tent – a soft secret world of its own within the hard brick and mortar surfaces of a house. Tenting is the furthest one can go in using fabric in interior decoration and we have accounts of some magnificent tents of the past which we can use for inspiration.

The 17th-century Bedouin tent of Nadir Shah was made of scarlet cloth, lined with violet satin embroidered in gold and precious stones. Imagine how this must have looked on a cold starlit night with the flickering of the fire catching the glint of gold and the gleam of jewels.

Even more magnificent and elaborate was the wedding tent of Alexander the Great, a huge structure supported by pillars and crowned with golden eagles. On the inside the pillars held up an architrave with cross-beams covered in linen on which were painted coffers made to imitate a solid roof. From the centre were suspended veils of scarlet bordered with white, under which, presumably, the wedding bed was placed. The pillars at the four corners of the tent were palm trees made of gold, and intervening ones were golden vines bearing grapes of amethyst.

You can hardly go to these lengths, but it is possible to translate some of the ideas into materials that are more readily available. For example, use a pretty Indian cloth embroidered with sequins and glass jewels as a canopy for a dining area or bed.

There is no reason why you should not be inspired by Alexander's tent and cover

RIGHT *Fabric has been used to create a new environment within the hard shell of a room.*

44

beams, real or fake, in cloth. You could go further, as he did, and paint the intervals between the beams in colours or patterned decorations. Stencilling would be the ideal medium to use here, in bands of intertwining designs.

Tented rooms may sound excessive, and the task of creating them daunting, but if you see them as consisting of separate elements that can be assembled in stages (rather like a tent), the effects come within anyone's reach. It is a question of seeing the walls as a series of vertical surfaces and the ceiling as a horizontal lid. You can stretch, drape or gather almost any sort of fabric on any of these surfaces, or you can begin by using fabric more locally, perhaps as a first experimental step while you gather confidence.

What about a flexible fabric wall? The simplest way to change the proportions and shape of a room is to use screens as space dividers. The Japanese do this to perfection. They use lightweight wooden-framed screens to separate sleeping, eating and cooking areas. Throughout the day these are moved according to the use of space, and each re-positioning of the screen creates a new environment.

This screen treatment is ideal for one-room living. Take, as an example, a small single-room studio flat with a separate bathroom. You can introduce screens to enclose the sleeping area, to frame the sitting space, or to shut off the kitchen department.

Think of screens covered in fabrics: a collection of stretched red and white patchworks or a series of striped fabrics or bright, harmonizing colours which you can switch round at will, and you will begin to get the feel of an ever changing, three-dimensional picture.

Try curtaining as a room divider, making a softly draped wall instead of a solid one. This can look extremely effective if you use sheer fabrics: a dining area can be curtained off in this way and lit at night to form a mysterious and glamorous room in which to entertain guests. The lights can be switched off and the

ABOVE *A large open room can be split into smaller areas when need be with floating walls of fabric.*

curtains left pulled to hide the empty plates and glasses once the meal is over. During the day or less formal evenings the curtain can be kept pulled to one side so that the whole room can be seen. Heavy interlined curtains can be used as room dividers if a certain amount of privacy or insulation is needed.

Although covering an entire wall or walls with fabric is much more expensive than applying a coat of paint, a fabric covering will conceal cracks, poor surfaces and wood-chip wallpaper and disguise ugly proportions. Fabric mutes harsh acoustics and creates an undeniably luxurious atmosphere. You can

LEFT *Heavy pleated fabric adds a sculptural dimension to this room. The lengths of fabric are hemmed and then tacked up randomly along the walls.*

LEFT *Unlined curtaining can be used as a room divider in any kind of setting.*

either fix curtain rails all round the walls from which to hang the fabric, or you can pin the fabric to the wall for a neat, unfussy look. For this second method lengths of battening which act as stretcher frames are attached to the walls at ceiling and floor level, and you tack or staple the fabric to these. Pelmets of any type will carry a decorative shape around the room and conceal the means by which the fabric is hung.

Applying panels of stretched fabric to walls is rather like applying wallpaper, it is easier if you don't use a large regular pattern. Match-

LEFT *Fabric can be fitted tightly over walls, is easier to use than wallpaper and doesn't tear. Take advantage of the textural properties of cloth, besides the vast range of designs and colours.*

ing patterns with a deep repeat can be tricky when working with gathered fabric, too. Concentrate on textures if pattern matching seems too complicated. Blond linen or suede fabric walls look very sophisticated. Consider black PVC for a bathroom against a backdrop of white tiles.

If you are using patterned fabrics, choose one that won't be too difficult to match, such as obvious stripes or checks. Another possibility is to use a fabric that has a very large overall design, such as blossoming trees or vines, and make a bower of a room. Mix different patterns together as do the Japanese, a geometric with a floral in the same shades of blue and white, and paint any intervening woodwork to co-ordinate. Different patterns can also be used for a dado and the remaining section of the wall above.

Doors can be treated as an entity in their own right when it comes to decorating with fabric. If they are panelled, fit the fabric into the panels and leave the frames as a contrasting surround. If a door or doorway is to be curtained, mount a separate rail over the lintel so that the curtaining can be easily pulled back. Built-in cupboards are greatly enhanced with a covering of fabric. Fabric can also be hung behind the doors, with the wooden panels removed completely. An ugly but indispensable free-standing wardrobe can be hidden by attaching a curtain track along the top and hanging curtains over it.

If you have a suitable alcove, fabric can turn it into a cupboard. At its simplest a cased curtain is hung from a rod suspended across the alcove, but this rather makeshift type of cupboard can be treated more decoratively to look like a little pavilion. A hoop or frame of wood is attached to the wall, rather like a half-tester frame, with the supports, if any are needed, underneath. A curtain track can then be attached to the frame and curtains hung. A small 'roof' can be made for the pavilion by attaching a width of fabric to the frame, gathering it at the top and attaching the gathered section to the wall.

The same fabric design is scaled down for use below the dado rail.

Warm red felt, hung with holly and lit by candlelight, makes a welcoming sight.

51

This gathered effect can also be used to lower a ceiling to the ideal height for the proportions of the room and to hide cracks. A simple and inexpensive method is to string wires across the ceiling and gather the fabric on to each length of wire via a casing so that the fabric billows out in undulating folds. Any light behind the false ceiling will be filtered and diffused.

The wonderful thing about fabric walls, doors and ceilings is that they need not be permanent. Use muslin and ribbon swags to

RIGHT *Easy to put up in summer, the entire framework for this awning can be packed away in winter.*

ABOVE *A flap can be attached to the edge of an umbrella – foreign legion style – that will act as an additional sunshade or as a shield from the wind.*

make a decorative background for a wedding reception or a child's party. Think of an entrance hall hung with welcoming felt, candlelit at Christmas time. Tented rooms can be put up for a single event. Think of a billowing muslin tent held back at intervals with ribbons and surrounded by a maze of potted plants, or of a navy blue cotton tent with a ceiling decorated with glistening silver stars circling a sparkling crescent moon – and you are almost in the world of Nadir Shah.

WALL CURTAIN

The simplest way to cover the walls of a room is with curtaining hung from a track. In this bedroom widths of sheer fabric have been stitched together in sections which can be parted at the windows and doors. Mount the track at the top of the wall against the ceiling, or use a ceiling-mounted track if there is little room for a conventional system. Weights can be fitted into the corners and along the base of each hem to hold the fabric against the walls.

Making the curtain

Mount the curtain track all round the room at the top of the wall (see HEADINGS, TRACKS AND POLES). Decide where the breaks in the fabric will fall and measure the respective sections of the track. Choose the heading tape and work out the number of fabric widths needed for each section (see CHOOSING TAPE).

Measure from the track to the floor and cut out the fabric widths to the correct length, adding 10cm (4in) for the base turning and 1cm (⅜in) for the top allowance.

Pin, tack and stitch the fabric widths together into their respective sections with flat fell seams.

Turn under a double 2cm (¾in) hem along the side edges and a double 5cm (2in) hem along the base of each section, mitring the corners (see FOLDING MITRED CORNERS). Pin, tack and stitch in place.

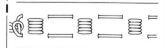

Turn down the top edge on each section for 1cm (⅜in). Cut a length of heading tape 10cm (4in)

longer than the section top. At one end, pull out the cords from the wrong side for 4cm (1½in) and knot together (**1**). Turn under the tape end for 1cm (⅜in) and pin the tape along the fabric 3mm (⅛in) from the curtain top. At the opposite side trim the tape, leaving a turn-under of 1cm (⅜in), and pull out the cords from the front of the tape. Tack and stitch the tape in place along both edges, working in the same direction. Stitch down the side edges, being careful not to catch the free cords with the needle.

To gather the fabric, hold the free cords in one hand and gently push the heading tape into evenly spaced pleats until the correct width is achieved

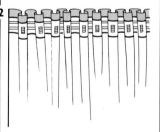

(**2**). Wind the surplus cords together and knot, but do not cut off. Fit hooks into the tape at about 8cm (3in) intervals and hang each section.

ABOVE *A sumptuous effect has been created by taking sheer curtains to the floor.*

WALL CURTAIN IDEAS

Evoke an oriental atmosphere by tacking a split bamboo cane grid on to the wall over a softly pleated curtain of glazed cotton or chintz. Use jade greens and ivory or tawny reds and golds to create a rich and exquisite effect. Or settle for a uniquely Japanese look by using lacquer-red fabric with black painted canes.

Filmy muslin dyed sugar pink is held together at the edges with rose pink ribbon. This is a simple and instant method of curtaining an uneven wall. You could even avoid using heading tapes and tracks by tacking lengths of beading across the top of the curtain to hold it in place.

DOOR CURTAIN

Cover the glass panel of a door with a sheer gathered curtain held in place by 1cm ($\frac{3}{8}$in) diameter brass rods slotted through a casing. Extra fabric is allowed on the length to produce the frills at the top and bottom of the curtain when it is gathered.

When using a fabric with a distinctive pattern, make sure the main motif is centred over the panel.

Making the curtain

Fix the rods in place at each side of the glass panel.

Decide on the fullness of the curtain – one and a half times the panel width should be sufficient. Add 4cm (1$\frac{1}{2}$in) to this measurement for side turnings. Next measure the length of the window and add 28cm (11in) to allow for the casings.

Cut one piece of fabric to these length and width dimensions.

Turn under a double 1cm ($\frac{3}{8}$in) hem down each side of the curtain. Pin, tack and stitch in place.

Fold under a double 7cm (2$\frac{3}{4}$in) hem along the top of the curtain; pin, tack and stitch in place close to the hem edge. Stitch across the hem again 3cm (1$\frac{1}{4}$in) up from the first row of stitching to form a casing for the rod (**1**).

Repeat to form a casing along the base edge of the curtain. Push the rods through the casings and hang the curtain.

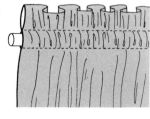

ABOVE *Match the fabric to the mood of the surroundings. Romantic lace would look good against plain stripped pine.*

57

FABRIC SCREEN

Fabric screens can be easily re-covered. Just remove the old coverings, hinges, tacks and nails, and sand down the wooden frame if necessary. Cover each panel separately with fabric, then re-hinge them together, positioning two hinges 10cm (4in) from the top and bottom edges and a third in between. The fabric can be held in place on the frame with decorative studs as here, or simply tacked in place. In this case, cover the tack heads with braid or painted wooden beading.

Cutting out the fabric
For the screen fronts, lay the fabric wrong side up. Place one wooden panel over the fabric with the panel edges parallel to the fabric selvedge. If the fabric is patterned, make sure the design is centred. Mark round the edges of the panel on to the fabric. Remove the panel and cut out the shape, adding a 1.5cm ($\frac{5}{8}$in) turn-under allowance all round (**1**). Using this fabric piece as a pattern, cut out the rest of the screen fronts.

For the screen backs, use a screen front piece as the pattern, adding the frame width all round when cutting out each back piece.

Covering the screen
Place the first back piece centrally to the first wooden panel. Pleat up the excess fabric at the base corners and tack the fabric in place (**2**).

At the side edges take the fabric round to the screen front and tack in place. Keep checking that the fabric is straight and taut before fixing. It can temporarily be held in place at the sides of the screen.

Make pleats where necessary to allow for the shaped top. Make sure that the pleats are evenly spaced and of equal amounts. Pin the pleats in place temporarily, then take the turning allowance round to the front edges and tack in position.

Turn under the edges on each front panel piece for 1.5cm ($\frac{5}{8}$in) and place the first piece centrally over a panel front, covering the raw edges of the back panel fabric. Fasten in place with evenly spaced decorative studs (**3**). The back of the screen can be studded to match in the same way if desired.

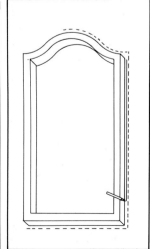

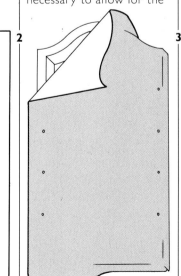

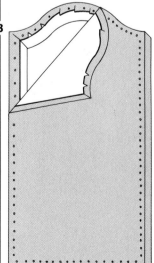

ABOVE *Besides screening off areas of a room, a fabric screen is a useful optional window covering.*

59

CONSERVATORY AWNING

Keep glaring sunlight at bay with gauzy panels of fabric stretched across the panes of a conservatory. They are supported by draw-strings slotted through side casings. Although the panels are normally kept in a closed position, they can be pushed back by hand.

Making the panels

Each ceiling panel is made to fit one window pane. Cream or white would be the best choice of colour for fabric that has to face the burning onslaught of the sun. Cut each panel to the correct width and length, adding a 5cm (2in) allowance to all sides for hems/casings.

Fold under a double 2.5cm (1in) hem at both ends of each panel; pin, tack and stitch the hems in place.

Fold under a double 2.5cm (1in) turning along each side edge to form the casing; pin, tack and stitch in place.

Thread fine cord through both casings and fasten the cord ends to an eyelet screw fixed into the wooden frame (**1**).

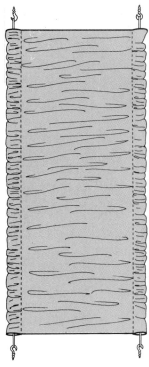

OUTSIDE AWNING

Making the awning
Measure the width of the position you want the awning to cover and add 8cm (3in) to this measurement for hems. Then decide on the depth of the awning overhang, allowing the circumference of the pole plus 2cm ($\frac{3}{4}$in) for casings along both edges. Cut or make up one piece of fabric to these dimensions.

Turn under a double 2cm ($\frac{3}{4}$in) hem along each side edge; pin, tack and stitch in place.

To make a casing along the top and bottom edges of the awning, turn under each edge for the required amount and then tuck under 1cm ($\frac{3}{8}$in). Pin, tack and stitch across the casing close to the raw edge foldline.

Slot lengths of dowel/bamboo through the casings (**1**). Place the poles over the top and bottom supports as shown.

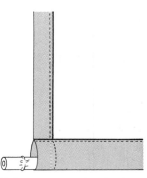

Make up an awning in the same way for each side. Hang as before, leaving the base pole unsupported.

Similar to a shop-front awning, this simplified version consists of bands of fabric held taut with lengths of dowel or bamboo inserted through casings along the top and bottom edges. The depth of the awning can equal the width of the fabric, avoiding the necessity of joining extra panels.

BELOW *This awning can be used over windows to keep out the glare as well as shading a patio area.*

TENTED ROOM

Disguise badly cracked walls and ceilings and turn a characterless and ill-proportioned room into a colourful, exotic tent. As in decorating, cover the ceiling first, then the walls, adding a fabric-covered band all round to hide the fixing tacks. If you use striped fabric, take care when cutting out that the stripes will follow the lines of the tent when the pieces are assembled. The fabric is held in place on 2cm by 2cm ($\frac{3}{4}$in by $\frac{3}{4}$in) battening fixed around the room.

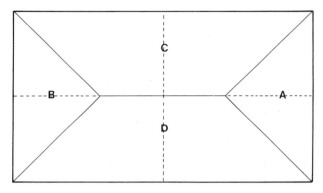

Covering the ceiling
First mark a line around the room at the level at which you wish the tented ceiling to hang.

Cut lengths of battening and fix it around the room at this height, spacing the screws at about 20cm (8in) intervals (**1**).

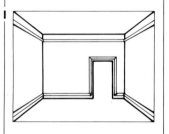

Mark the centre of the ceiling, then mark a line through this centre point that runs the length of the ceiling parallel to the walls. Mark off a distance of about 60cm (24in) on either side of the centre point – this measurement will depend on the length of the room.

Measure the distance from the end of the marked line to the room corners to obtain the length of the diagonal sides of section A. Measure the straight side from corner to corner. Cut a paper pattern of this section. Repeat to make a

pattern for section B; then make patterns for the four-sided sections, C and D. Check that the pattern pieces fit together.

From the fabric, cut out each section, adding a seam allowance of 1.5cm ($\frac{5}{8}$in) to the diagonal and short inner edges and 2cm ($\frac{3}{4}$in) to the outer edges to allow for fixing. If necessary, join fabric pieces together to gain the width of a section, spacing the seams evenly.

With right sides together and raw edges even, pin, tack and stitch the four-sided sections together along the inner edges. Cut two 12cm (5in) lengths of narrow tape and fold in half to form loops.

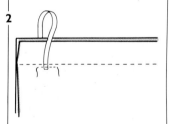

On the wrong side of the fabric stitch the loops either side of the inner edge seam following the previous stitching (**2**). Pin, tack and stitch the three- and four-sided sections together to form a

large rectangle.

Screw two cup hooks into the ceiling that will match up with the loops. Hook up the fabric ceiling.

Working from the centre of each wall, tack the fabric to the battening, keeping it taut and matching seams to corners.

Covering the walls
Fix battening vertically at the corners, along the top of the skirting and around the doors and windows, leaving a gap of about 3mm ($\frac{1}{8}$in) between the battening and these fixtures.

Next measure the length and width of each wall in turn. Cut out the amount of fabric widths needed to fit each wall, allowing 1.5cm ($\frac{5}{8}$in) for seams and 2cm ($\frac{3}{4}$in) for tuck-ins or fixing along all the outer edges. Join widths together with plain flat seams.

Tack the top edge of each fabric piece to the battening around the edge of the room. At the windows and doors simply push the fabric edges in between the battening and the fixtures. At the base of the walls push the fabric edges in between the

battening and skirting (**3**).

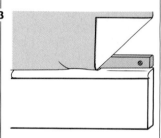

Covering the battening
Make up a strip of fabric the width of each wall by 53cm (21in). Fold the strip in half lengthways, right sides together. Pin, tack and stitch into a long tube, taking a 1.5cm ($\frac{5}{8}$in) seam allowance. Trim and turn to the right side. Press the tube flat with the seam to the centre back.

Cut a length of 2.5cm (1in) thick foam the same length and width as the tube. Push the foam inside the tube. Position the foam-filled tube centrally to the battening, and hand stitch in place to the ceiling and walls. At the corners turn in the raw edges of fabric and slipstitch together, trimming the foam so the fabric edges butt together.

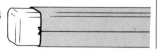

ABOVE *Create a world of your own, a room within a room, from fabric. Just think of a theme and choose the fabric that best expresses it.*

63

WINDOWS

Windows are the eyes of the house and frame your view of the world. They also let others see in. They may be architectural features worth looking at in themselves, or functional necessities that you simply look through. They need by definition to be flexible – to open and close, exclude daylight or block draughts, and to look good while performing any of these functions. This mixture of the practical and the aesthetic influences how you dress your windows. Whether you want something to insulate, to block, to filter or to maximize the amount of daylight in the room, to provide privacy; whether you choose to make the window a dominant feature or understate its presence. See the window and its treatment as a whole: the range of fabrics, styles and hardware is so immense that you can permute the possibilities to make a window for all seasons.

But if the view is beautiful and you are not overlooked, do you need fabric at all? Treat the window like a picture, and leave it bare. If you do need to soften the frame, take your cue from the landscape, perhaps following the example of the house overlooking a lake which was forever changing from blues to greys to greens. The large windows were hung with shimmering greeny-blue fabric and the rest of the room echoed these colours, too, so that it felt almost part of the outside.

The extremes of day and night make every window into a transformation scene, and the most enchanting daytime view becomes a pool of blackness at night. Even when no one can look in, you may want to soften the stark blackness of the panes with a gauzy veil, or a

RIGHT *The light throws these fabric shapes into dramatic relief, highlighting their weave and making the colours glow. When there is no need for windows to be completely curtained, try experimenting with unusually shaped coverings.*

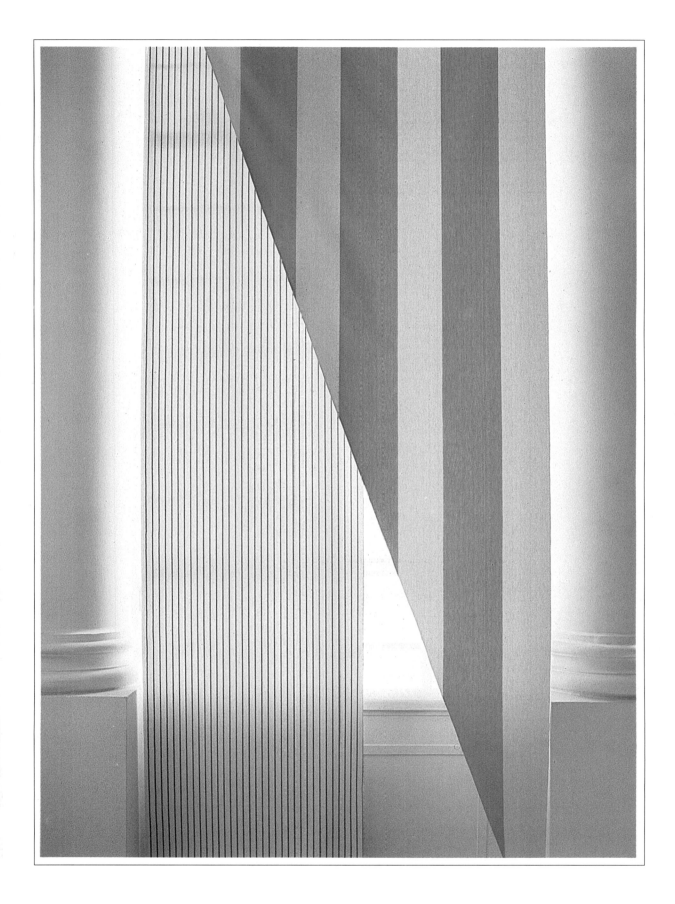

Inexpensive and fun, a Chinese paper kite serves as an improvised blind.

length of lace whose pattern will exploit the contrast.

Whatever the window calls for, try to make your response positive. You may need privacy but want to make the most of the light available. The conventional net curtains slung across the window at half-mast is the unimaginative response to this situation. Instead consider a translucent paper screen that comes halfway up the window, a roller blind pulled upwards to intercept the gaze of the passers-by – or give them something to look at, such as a Chinese paper kite shaped like a fish. Maximize light inside the room with mirrors lining the window recess.

RIGHT A simple window is complemented by a sheer curtain that does not fight with the view beyond. The stencilling echoes the leafy view and frames the curtain.

RIGHT Privacy and protection from the light are good reasons for covering this magnificent window. The gauzy fabric does not obscure the shape of the window and the pleating draws attention to the curve.

Too little light, or too much. Perhaps you need a complete black-out in order to sleep: it is the density of fabric rather than colour that best achieves this. Line curtains with special black-out interlining or devise a combination of blinds and curtains, so that this requirement doesn't interfere with and darken the room's own colour scheme. Perhaps you need to keep light from fading delicate furnishings: gauze curtains make a shield against the glare of the sun, but you can present this necessity in an ingenious and creative way by including it as part of a multi-layered window

treatment. Not only is there a huge choice of fabric designs, but these can be combined in textural or patterned layers at the window – blinds plus curtains, drapes with blinds, and layers of different weights of curtaining.

Individual touches in the presentation can transform the most basic curtains into something special. There is no need to stick to furnishing textiles, either. A length of taffeta knotted to one side of the window by day looks sumptuous and has style. Drifting saris are graceful. Felt drapes well, looks warm, comes in glowing colours and doesn't have to be hemmed. The simplest curtains are just wound loosely round the pole without any hems or lining. The draped coils can be secured at the back of the pole with staples or a few stitches. Sheets, shawls and tablecloths make instant curtaining. During the day they can slide back along the pole or be lifted up at the corner. Next in simplicity come unlined curtains, with the minimum of sewing to attach tapes or ribbon loops at the top. There is no reason why the widths should not drift independently of one another, as unlined curtains are not intended primarily to keep out draughts or cold. Make a feature of this, or pierce the sides with eyelets and lash them together with ribbons.

When making classic gathered curtains, though, never skimp on the width, otherwise they look mean however good the fabric. Enjoy the lining: use a bright colour that glows through cream or white sheer curtains, or choose a minimal sprigged or striped print that tones with the main fabric – and then hook back the curtains to show off the 'wrong' sides. (Avoid using precious fabric for the lining, though, since it takes a good deal of wear from sunlight.) Both top and bottom of curtains provide opportunities for decorative impact. At the bottom the curtain could just fall in draped folds on the floor, be bound or frilled or shaped into scallops. Handmade headings offer alternatives to bought tapes. (Curtains are often clustered into pleats at the top, but why not have them

LEFT Grey flannel and glossy browny red paintwork make a sophisticated colour mix and provide textural interest. The soft drape of the curtains provides a good contrast with the spare lines of the furniture.

Both top and bottom of these curtains have scalloped edges – this can be done either by machine or hand.

accordion pleated all the way down by a specialist firm? It takes about three times the track width of fabric – but even muslin is effective; taffeta or watered silk would be as enticing as a ballgown.)

For maximum decorative effect, consider using curtains in several layers. Begin with an abundant layer of net or gauze that puffs out subsequent fabrics. Then add a silk or lightweight cotton, plain or minimally patterned; finally, top these with a heavier plain or large-patterned fabric. Let the layers be pulled back at staggered intervals. A combined valance and curtain track could hold the first two layers, with the heavier fabric draped over a pole and dropping down in tails at the sides. A more restrained and less expensive draped effect is to team a roller

RIGHT *Two differently shaped pelmets make the most of a floral fabric.*

RIGHT *Pelmets looks good on their own without curtains, or they can be teamed with a roller blind. Treat the window as a picture that can be given a frame or filled in like a blank canvas.*

ABOVE *What could be a
stark room has been made to
seem warm by covering the
windows to produce a gentle
diffused light.*

blind with a curtain length swathed along a pole and reaching the floor on either side – the draping can continue right around a bay.

They not only take far less fabric than curtains, but roller blinds are very adaptable and suit both modern and traditional settings. They work best in a firm, close weave, but spray stiffener can give body to gauzy fabrics – even lace. Roller blinds make perfect blank canvases on which to try out painted effects, and the base edge can be shaped.

Roman blinds look best in sheets of solid colour or uncluttered printed fabrics. Their image is more elegant than that of roller blinds, and they are better at blocking draughts, since they can be made from much thicker fabric and can be lined as well. Lining can become a feature if it extends beyond the edges like a binding.

Austrian blinds were originally designed for tall windows and can look foolish on small ones. For a change from the usual frilly look, make them in plain fabric or clean blue and white stripes. If no frill is attached, they will look like a curtain when let down. An Austrian blind also makes a good festoon pelmet over a plain expanse of roller blind and – if corded only across the middle – will form tails at either side when pulled up.

The finishing touches are the pelmets, valances and swags, the tie-backs – and the

ABOVE *Austrian and roller blinds combine well. The two layers can be used separately or together.*

choice of the hardware of poles, rings and pulls. Since these elements can add firm lines to echo the architecture or a soft framework of folds to set off the fabric at the windows, they should be planned at the outset as part of one coherent design – although it might eventually take a fair amount of adjustment and experimentation to get the drapes right *in situ*. However sumptuous or minimal your windows (and the choice is, as always, entirely personal), one rule remains: keep the glass clean!

LEFT *Curtaining can be treated like clothing fabric. This cloth has been accordian pleated. A fat bow draws the curtain into the window centre rather than to the side.*

LEFT and BELOW *Anything that is long enough can be used as a tie-back – from garlands of flowers to chains, beads and strung shells.*

MEASURING UP – CURTAINS

Before you measure for curtains the track or pole should be in position (see HEADINGS, TRACKS AND POLES). An expandable metal rule gives a more accurate measurement than a fabric tape and is easier to use.

Calculating the length

Generally curtains look best floor or sill length, but, depending on the look of the curtains relative to the window, any convenient length in between will do. It is also possible to allow the bottom of the curtains to drape into folds on the floor.

Decide how long you would like your curtains, measuring the length from the top of the track or just underneath the pole as shown. Then add the allowances for the hem and heading (see HEADINGS). For floor- or sill-length curtains, deduct 1cm ($\frac{3}{8}$in) from the length measurement to allow the curtains to just clear the floor or sill.

Calculating the width

The number of fabric widths needed to cover a window is determined by the length of the track or pole and the style of curtain heading you choose. Some headings require a large amount of fabric and others much less. Many of the headings in the following chapter are handmade and the fullness of fabric required is indicated in the instructions; other headings are produced by using commercial heading tape and the fullness required for each type is given in HEADINGS, TRACKS AND POLES.

To calculate the total number of widths required, multiply the fabric fullness by the track or pole length. Then divide this amount by a single fabric width, rounding up to the nearest whole number. For divided curtains halve this amount to get the number of widths that have to be joined to make one of a pair. Attach any half-widths to the outer edge of each curtain.

HEADINGS, TRACKS AND
POLES   206

HEADINGS, TRACKS AND
POLES   206

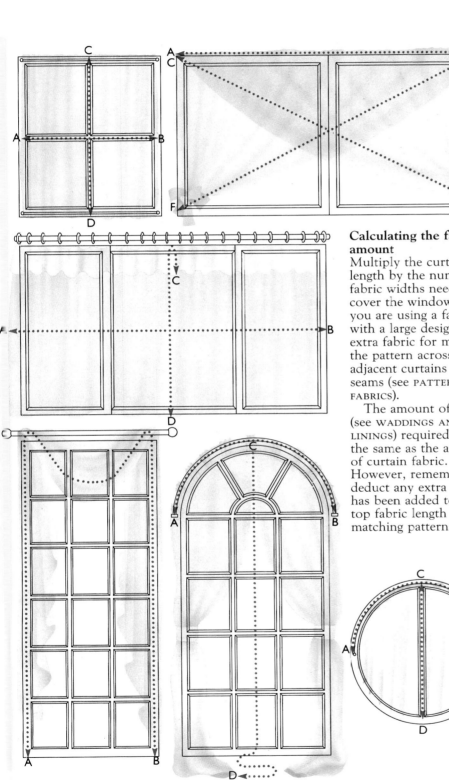

Calculating the fabric amount

Multiply the curtain length by the number of fabric widths needed to cover the window. If you are using a fabric with a large design allow extra fabric for matching the pattern across adjacent curtains and seams (see PATTERNED FABRICS).

The amount of lining (see WADDINGS AND LININGS) required will be the same as the amount of curtain fabric. However, remember to deduct any extra that has been added to the top fabric length for matching patterns.

Cutting out

Lay the prepared fabric flat, making sure any one-way design or pile is facing in the right direction.

Straighten the bottom edge (see PREPARING TO SEW) and measure off the first curtain length. Rule a straight cutting line across the fabric in pencil or tailor's chalk, lining up a square-cornered object like a book against the selvedge to obtain a right angle. Cut along the marked line. Cut out any subsequent lengths in the same way. See PATTERNED FABRICS for instructions on cutting out curtain lengths with a large printed or woven design.

To obtain curtain half-widths, fold one width in half lengthways, pinning selvedge to selvedge, and cut along the fold with sharp scissors.

Snip into the curtain selvedges to release the tightly woven edge before hemming or stitching.

DRAPED SHEER CURTAINS

These curtains with their centre draped section are cleverly made in one piece. The curtains are attached at the top to the central section and casings prevent them from slipping off the pole. Make the curtains floor length or extra long so they drift into folds.

Making the curtains

Measure for the curtains (see MEASURING UP), adding the circumference of the pole plus 8cm (3in) for the hem and seam allowances to the length.

To measure for the centre draped section fix a length of string at one end of the pole, let it hang down for the required amount, and then fix it at the opposite end of the pole. This distance should equal the long front edge of the draped section. The length of the short back edge should equal the width between the two curtains plus 46cm (18in). The length of each side should be the same as the full curtain width.

Make up two curtains from the fabric to the required width, joining any widths together with flat fell seams. Turn under a double 2cm ($\frac{3}{4}$in) hem along the sides and a double 3cm (1$\frac{1}{4}$in) hem along the base, mitring the corners (see FOLDING MITRED CORNERS). Pin, tack and stitch the hems in place.

Make up a paper pattern for the draped section allowing for double 1cm ($\frac{3}{8}$in) hems along the front and back and a 1.5cm ($\frac{5}{8}$in) seam at each side.

Cut out the centre section. Turn under a double 1cm ($\frac{3}{8}$in) hem on the front and back edges and pin, tack and stitch in place. Pin, tack and stitch the right side of the top of each curtain (**1**) to the wrong side of the centre section at the side edges. Fold each curtain at this point so the foldline is the pole circumference measurement plus 2cm ($\frac{3}{4}$in) from the seam. Pin, tack and stitch along the curtain to form a casing.

Thread the curtain pole through each casing in turn (**2**), then bring the centre draped section over the pole to the front (**3**).

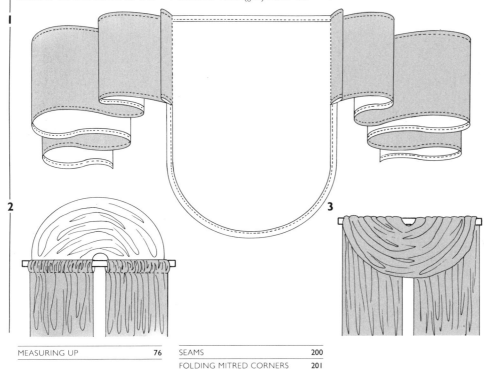

ABOVE *With the right treatment sheer curtains can look glamorous and elegant besides being functional.*

WRAPPING THE POLE

Where there is no necessity to cover a window with folds of curtaining, outline the frame with fabric instead. A swathed pole and one fabric width of curtaining is all that is needed. After covering the pole and knobbed ends with fabric, drape the false curtain over the pole in sweeping loops of fabric. Alternatively simply wrap the fabric in loose coils round the pole and hang a pair of conventional curtains behind.

Covering the pole

Position the brackets for the pole above the window (see HEADINGS, TRACKS AND POLES).

For each knob cut a circle of fabric, the diameter of which should be slightly larger than the circumference of the knob. Place the wrong side of the fabric over the knob and wrap the fabric round, pleating it evenly. Pin the pleats, then either stick or staple them in position. It may be necessary to hand stitch the pleats to hold them firmly (**1**).

Cut a piece of fabric the length of the pole plus 4cm (1½in) by the circumference plus 4cm (1½in). Wrap the fabric around the pole so that it overlaps. Turn under 2cm (¾in) along the length and hand stitch it in place. Turn under 2cm (¾in) at each end and hand stitch

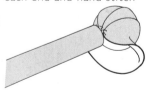

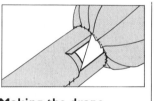

in place to the pleated section (**2**).
Place the pole above the window with the seam at the back.

Making the drape

Using a length of string, measure for the draped section. Wrap the string round the pole, making loops down to the top of the window, and let it dangle to the floor on both sides, remembering to allow extra for floor draping (**3**).
Cut one fabric width to this length. Cut and join more widths if a very full drape is required. Turn under a double 1cm (⅜in) hem along the side edges and a double 5cm (2in) hem along the ends,

mitring the corners (see FOLDING MITRED CORNERS).

Tack and stitch the hems in place.

Mark where the curtaining will drape over the pole at one of the outer edges and work two rows of gathering stitches across the fabric at this position. Gather this section to half the fabric width and fasten off.

Cut a strip of touch and close fastening to the same length as the gathering. Pin, tack and stitch one half to the underside of the curtaining over the gathering stitches (**4**).

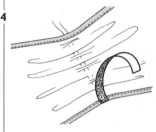

Stitch the opposite half of the fastening along the pole. Repeat the procedure for the other end of the pole. Next gather up the drape where it crosses the pole at the centre but to only two thirds of the fabric width. Attach touch and close fastening as before.

Drape the fabric over the pole, pressing the fastening strips together.

ABOVE *Simple, but effective, this draped and wrapped curtaining explodes the myth that curtain poles look severe.*

BELOW *If the other pole wrapping treatment is too powerful, try this more muted but no less elegant version.*

Method II

Cover the pole as before. Drape the string in loose coils around the pole as shown (**1**). Cut one fabric width to the string measurement and turn under a double 1cm ($\frac{3}{8}$in) hem all round. Fasten one end of the fabric behind the covered pole, then coil it loosely around the pole before fastening in place at the opposite side (**2**).

Make up two curtains to fit the window in the usual way (see MEASURING UP) and hang behind the pole on a conventional curtain track.

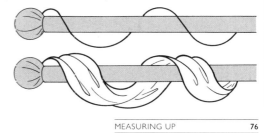

MEASURING UP   76

81

UNLINED CURTAINS

Fix a curtain pole high above a curved window and hang it with curtains with a deep floppy heading. Choose a fabric with body so the top pleats and base folds will hang well. This gives the curtains a substantial look that is usually only achieved with linings and interlinings.

BELOW *Extra-long length, a brass pole and a plump, deep heading add up to a dramatic theatrical look that belies the fact that these are simple unlined curtains.*

Making the curtains
Measure up for the curtains (see MEASURING UP), allowing 40cm (16in) for the heading and an extra 50cm (20in) for draping over the floor. The fabric fullness required for these curtains is one and a half to two times the pole length.

Turn under a double 2cm (¾in) hem along the side edges and a double 5cm (2in) hem along the base of each curtain, mitring the corners (see FOLDING MITRED CORNERS). Pin, tack and slip hem all round the curtains.

At the top of each curtain, turn 40cm (16in) to the wrong side; turn under 1cm (⅜in) along the raw edge and pin, tack and stitch across the curtain.

Divide the curtain into equal sections, making marks at the base of the hemmed top about 20cm (8in) apart. Stitch a curtain ring to the curtain at each mark. Thread the rings on to the curtain pole and bend down the curtain top to the right side (**1**).

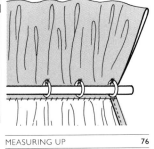

SHEER UNLINED CURTAIN

Used with panache, uncluttered sheer curtains have many more decorative possibilities than their rather practical image suggests. Choose from an enormous variety of textures, patterns and fibres in natural or white. Stitch a simple cased heading, as shown here, and slot through a covered wire.

BELOW *Few fabrics lend themselves so well to a high-tech environment as the cool elegance of a sheer fabric.*

Making the curtain
Measure for the curtain (see MEASURING UP), allowing twice the wire length for fullness. Cut out the required number of fabric widths and join them together with flat fell seams.

Turn under a double 1cm ($\frac{3}{8}$in) hem along the side edges and a double 4cm ($1\frac{1}{2}$in) hem along the base, mitring the corners (see FOLDING MITRED CORNERS). Pin, tack and stitch.

At the top of the curtain turn under a double 6cm ($2\frac{1}{2}$in) hem along the top edge. Pin, tack and stitch close to the hem edge. Stitch another row of stitching across the curtain top 2.5cm (1in) above the first row to form a casing. Slot the wire through the casing and hang the curtain. The fabric above the casing will gather into a frill (**1**).

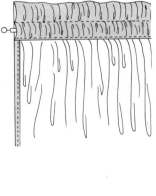

CROSS-OVER SHEER CURTAINS

Two lengths of sheer curtaining have been crossed over a set of undercurtains then draped over white ceramic door knobs fixed beside the window. Attached to the top of the cross-over sections are tape ties which are knotted through the eyelets on the wooden curtain rings that hold up the undercurtains.

Making the undercurtains

Measure for the undercurtains (see MEASURING UP), allowing twice the track width for fullness. Stitch any fabric widths together with flat fell seams.

Turn under a double 2cm (¾in) hem along the side edges and a 5cm (2in) double hem along the base, mitring the corners (see FOLDING MITRED CORNERS).

At the top edge turn under a double 2cm (¾in) hem, making neat top corners. Pin, tack and stitch in place.

Mark out the pleat positions along the top of the fabric at 26cm (10in) intervals. At each mark, fold a 1cm (⅜in) deep pleat (**1**). Pin, tack and stitch down the back of the pleat for 10cm (4in).

Hand stitch a hook behind each pleat and slot through the eyelets on the curtain rings to hang the curtains.

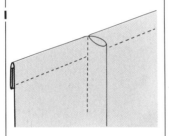

Making the tape-tied curtains

Measure the length of the curtains by tying a length of string to the pole at the desired position and draping it across the window and over one of the knobs to the floor.

Cut two one-fabric-width curtains to this length, allowing 8cm (3¼in) for the hem and top turning on each curtain. Turn under a double 1cm (⅜in) hem along the side edges and a double 3cm (1¼in) hem along the base, mitring the corners as explained before.

Cut out the required amount of 30cm (12in) lengths of 1cm (⅜in) wide tape for the ties. Place them in pairs one on top of the other along the top

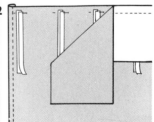

raw edge of the curtain at 15cm (6in) intervals, beginning and ending with a pair at each side edge (**2**).

Make up a 5cm (2in) wide facing the same length as the curtain width. Place the facing to the curtain top over the ties with right sides together and matching raw edges. Pin, tack and stitch in place, taking a 2cm (¾in) seam allowance. Turn the facing to the wrong side and press under 1.5cm (⅝in) along the base and side edges. Pin, tack and stitch in place.

Thread the ties through the ring eyelets from either side and knot. Cross over the curtains and hook round the door knobs fixed to the wall for tie-backs.

CURTAIN IDEAS

With a little imagination and a minimum of sewing you can create some dazzling effects with pairs of sheer curtains. Combine glowing colours such as apricot with white, or ice blue with mint green. By hanging a pair of triangular curtains with casings on two sides you can achieve an unusual diagonal design.

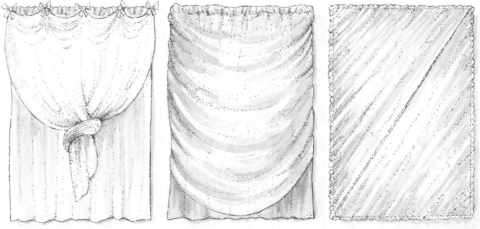

ABOVE *The cross-over
section of this window
treatment can be added to
any set of basic curtains.*

LINED CURTAINS

Give your curtains a professional finish and ensure that they remain looking marvellous for a long time. The best way of achieving a luxuriant draped look is to lockstitch the top fabric and lining together at intervals down the curtain length. Choose a lining colour that matches the fabric or a tone that harmonizes with the façade of the house.

Adding a layer of interlining between the curtain and lining gives extra body and makes the curtains extremely durable, while increasing their insulating properties. Box, cartridge or triple pleat heading tapes are particularly suitable for heavy lined curtains.

Making up the curtain widths

Measure up for the curtains (see MEASURING UP) and cut out the curtain and lining lengths.

Pin, tack and stitch the curtain fabric widths together with plain flat seams; repeat for the lining widths. Fold a single 6.5cm (2½in) hem along the side edges of each curtain and a single 15cm (6in) hem along the base, mitring the corners (see FOLDING MITRED CORNERS). If curtain weights are necessary, they should be added at this stage (see HEADINGS, TRACKS AND POLES). Herringbone stitch down the side edges and along the base to hold the hem in place.

Marking the lockstitching rows

Lay the curtains flat, wrong sides up, and mark the positions for the lockstitching rows. Using a metre (yard) stick and tailor's chalk or marking pen, draw down the centre of each curtain from top to hem. Mark parallel lines 30cm (12in) apart across the curtain width.

Attaching the lining

Position the lining over the curtain fabric with wrong sides together and matching top raw edges. Pin the curtain and lining together down the centre line. Fold back the lining against the line of pins and, using a thread that matches the curtain, lockstitch the two fabrics together from the top edge to the top of the curtain hem (**1**). Fold the lining back over the curtain and pin together down the next marked line, then lockstitch the fabrics together as before.

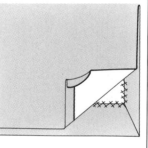

Repeat at each marked line, working both ways from the centre.

Tack the two fabrics together along the top edge. Trim the lining down to match the folded side and base edges of the top fabric. Turn under 2cm (¾in) along the side edges of the lining and 5cm (2in) along the base, folding neat corners. Pin and tack the lining to the hemmed edges of the curtain; slip hem the lining to the curtain.

2

Attaching the heading tape

Treating the top fabric and lining as one at the top edge, attach the chosen heading tape (see HEADINGS, TRACKS AND POLES).

ABOVE *Softly draped, lined curtains will soften hard angles and change the proportions of archway or window.*

87

LACE INSET CURTAINS

Make up these curtains to exactly fit the window – omitting a heading tape or hand gathers. Choose a lace that will blend in well with the background fabric and, if desired, add a matching lace edging to the side edges of the curtains.

Making the basic curtains

Fix a brass rod into the ceiling recess (see HEADINGS, TRACKS AND POLES). Measure off the desired length of the curtains from the rod and measure the rod width. Cut two pieces of fabric for the curtains. Each one should equal half the rod width plus 4cm (1½in) for side turnings by the desired length plus 6cm (2½in) for the hem minus about 25cm (10in) for the lace top (this will depend on the size of the window and design of lace).

Turn under a double 1cm (⅜in) hem along the sides and a double 3cm (1¼in) hem along the base, mitring the corners (see FOLDING MITRED CORNERS). Pin, tack and stitch in place.

Make up a paper pattern for the decorative top edge. Position it to the top edge of the curtain 6mm (¼in) from raw edge and mark on to the fabric (1).

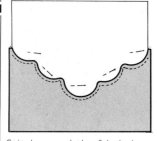

Stitch round the fabric just outside the marked edge. Cut out around the shaped

top, then zigzag stitch around the cut-out shape.

Positioning the lace insets

Make up two pieces of lace each the same width as one of curtains plus 2cm (¾in) on each side by the required length plus 3cm (1¼in). Turn under double 1cm (⅜in) wide side hems; pin, tack and stitch. Position the curtain right side up and place the lace

so that it overlaps the top edge by 1cm (⅜in) and the side edges match (2). Pin, tack and straight stitch close to the edge of the lace. At the top edge of curtain turn over a double 1cm (⅜in) wide hem; pin, tack and stitch in place.

Stitch the curtain top to the eyelets at the base of the rings at equally spaced intervals across the curtain top. Thread the rings onto the brass rod.

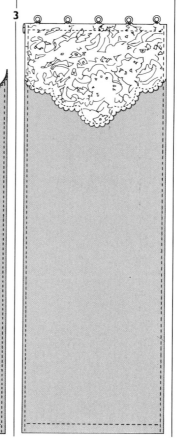

ABOVE *Highlight the decorative aspect of a room with a touch of lace.*

THREE CURTAIN IDEAS

BELOW *Concentrate on the heading to make simple unlined curtains look special.*

Pick a contrasting fabric to highlight a plain top. Gather the top of a curtain and create a cosy country look with the addition of some wooden beading. Link together pairs of plain curtains with a length of fabric wound through the curtain rings on to which the curtains are tied.

RIGHT *Loop lengths of self-fabric across a backdrop of continuous curtaining.*

BELOW *Just lift these curtains to one side and secure if more light is needed.*

Contrast edging

Make up a 5cm (2in) wide length of contrast fabric to fit the top edge of the ungathered curtain. Turn down the top edge of the curtain to the right side by 1cm ($\frac{3}{8}$in). Turn under 1cm ($\frac{3}{8}$in) on all edges of the contrast strip and place to the curtain top so that the folded edges at the top butt together (**1**). Pin, tack and stitch the contrast fabric in place.

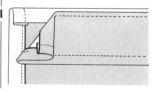

Attach a curtain heading tape (see HEADINGS, TRACKS AND POLES) in the usual way to the top of the curtain. Depending on the width of the heading tape, it may be possible to combine the stitching on the binding with stitching on the tape (**2**).

Gathers and beading

Fix a length of 2cm ($\frac{3}{4}$in) wide battening across the complete window area. After making up each curtain turn over the top edge to the wrong side for 17cm (7in), then turn under the raw edge for 1cm ($\frac{3}{8}$in) and work two rows of gathering stitches along the hem edge through all thicknesses (**1**).

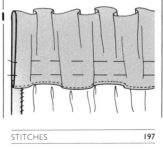

Pull up to fit the batten over the window and temporarily fasten in place with tacks at about 30cm (12in) intervals (**2**). Tease out the gathers until they are evenly spaced across the batten and then hammer tacks in place at about 10cm (4in) intervals.

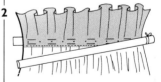

Cut a length of rounded beading to fit the window width and hang over the gathered curtains on brackets.

HEADINGS, TRACKS AND POLES   206

STITCHES   197

Fabric ties and loops

Make up as many pairs of ties as needed to cover the top edge of the curtain, spacing them at 20cm (8in) intervals.

For each tie cut a piece of fabric 5cm by 22cm (2in by 9in). Fold the fabric in half with right sides together; pin, tack and stitch the long edges, taking a 1cm ($\frac{3}{8}$in) seam allowance. Press the seam to the centre and stitch across one end. Trim and turn to the right side.

Make up a 5cm (2in) wide facing for the top edge of the curtain, stitching fabric widths together if necessary. Turn under 1.5cm ($\frac{5}{8}$in) along the base edge of the facing; pin and tack. Position the raw ends of the ties in pairs to the right side of the curtain top at equally spaced intervals, placing a pair at each side edge. With right sides together, place the facing to the curtain edge over the ties; pin, tack and stitch across the top, taking a 1.5cm ($\frac{5}{8}$in) seam allowance. Trim the seam and turn the facing to wrong side. Turn in the side edges and slipstitch. Stitch the base edge of the facing in place.

At 2cm ($\frac{3}{4}$in) from each tie, make a 1cm ($\frac{3}{8}$in) tuck to the front of the curtain. Pin, tack and stitch the two fabric thicknesses together for 4cm (1$\frac{1}{2}$in). The tucks should stand out from the curtain (**1**).

Hem the raw edges of one fabric width – the length will depend on the window size – and thread through odd curtain rings along the entire length of the curtain, making large loops of fabric as shown.

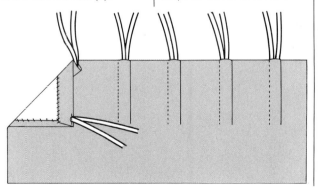

SIX CURTAIN HEADINGS

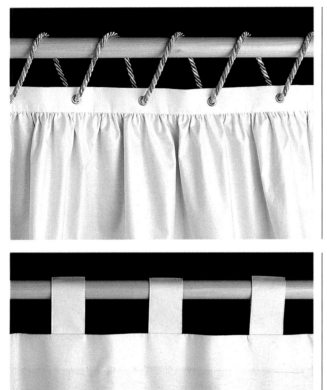

Eyelet heading

Cut an 11cm (4¼in) wide piece of fabric equal to the finished curtain width. Cut a length of iron-on interfacing half the width of the fabric band minus 1.5cm (⅝in) seam allowance. Bond to the wrong side, placing the interfacing within the seamline. Fold the fabric band in half with right sides together; stitch across both ends. Trim and turn.

Gather up the curtain. Place one long edge of the band to the gathered top edge of the curtain with right sides together and raw edges even; stitch, taking a 1.5cm (⅝in) seam allowance. Turn under the remaining edge.

Fix the eyelets in position along the band and fasten over a pole with cord.

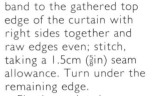

Looped heading

For each loop cut two pieces of fabric 8cm by 23cm (3in by 9in). Pin the fabric pieces together with right sides facing and stitch the side edges. Trim and turn to the right side.

Fold each loop in half and pin the raw edges to the top raw edge of curtain, placing a loop at each hemmed side edge and the rest at 15cm (6in) intervals in between.

Make up a 6.5cm (2½in) wide facing to the same width as the curtain. Stitch to the curtain top. Trim and turn to the wrong side. Turn in the side and base edges.

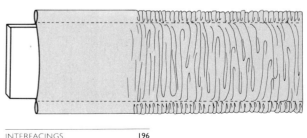

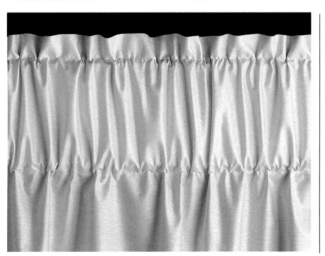

Wide cased heading

After stitching the side hems, turn the curtain top to the wrong side for 14cm (5½in). Tuck under the raw edge for 1cm (⅜in) and stitch across the curtain. Stitch across the curtain again 2.5cm (1in) from the top folded edge, forming a 10.5cm (4⅛in) wide casing and top decorative edge. Slot a flat curtain rod through the casing to gather the curtain.

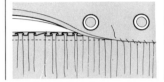

Pleated heading

Turn over the top edge of the curtain for 4cm (1½in). Turn under the raw edge for 1cm (⅜in) and hand stitch. Mark the top of the curtain for inverted pleats with foldlines 6.5cm (2½in) on each side of placement lines (see PLEATS). Pleat the curtain top; pin and tack to hold. Stitch across the pleats 5cm (2in) down from top edge. Cut out triangles of bonding fabric. Position one triangle over the stitching and one on each side of the pleat as shown. Bond in place. Stitch round each triangle. Sew rings behind each pleat.

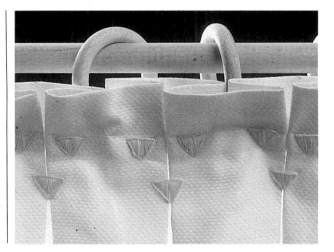

Shirred heading

Make up the desired amount of 1cm (⅜in) wide self-fabric ties. Place the ties together in pairs along the top of the curtain. Make up a 8.5cm (3½in) wide facing to fit the curtain width. With right sides together and raw edges even, attach the facing to the curtain top. Work six rows of shirring spaced about 6mm (¼in) apart across the curtain top, but do not stitch through the facing. Pull up each row to the required length and fasten off. Fold down the facing over the back of the shirring. Turn in the side and base edges. Alternatively, you can turn under a double 6mm (¼in) hem along the curtain top, work the rows of shirring, and then stitch the ties to the wrong side of the curtain.

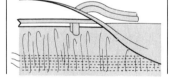

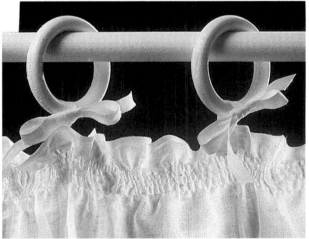

Velvet-trimmed heading

After hemming the sides, turn the top edge of curtain to the wrong side for 9cm (3½in). Turn under the raw edge for 1cm (⅜in) and tack across the curtain. Slipstitch the folded side edges of the top hem together. Work two rows of gathering stitches across the curtain through both layers of fabric just above the hem edge. Pull up the gathers evenly to the required width and fasten off. Stitch across the gathers to hold, catching in the hem. Place a 2.5cm (1in) wide velvet ribbon centrally over the rows of gathering and tack in place close to the side edges in order not to mark the velvet; turn under the ends. Stitch the ribbon in place.

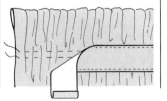

MEASURING UP – PELMETS

The first step in measuring for a pelmet is to fix the support board above the window.

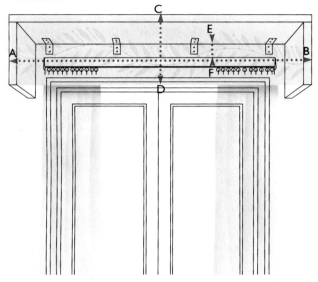

Fitting the board
The board is a 10cm (4in) wide shelf cut from 1.5cm to 2cm ($\frac{5}{8}$in–$\frac{3}{4}$in) thick plywood. Position it between 5cm (2in) and 8cm (3in) above the window. It should project at least 5cm (2in) either side of the curtain track. Place small brackets at each end and then space them at 30cm (12in) intervals in between. Nail a 10cm (4in) square of plywood across each end. If the pelmet is deep, it may be necessary to fix a length of hardboard in front of the shelf to give the pelmet extra backing.

Calculating the pelmet size
For the pelmet width measure the length of the board and add 20cm (8in) for the returns (the sections between the front of the board and the wall). Decide on the depth, taking into account how the pelmet will look in proportion to the curtain.

Cut the fabric, stiffener and lining to the correct size and shape. Centre a complete fabric width and attach side panels if widths have to be joined to cover a wide pelmet.

Patterned fabrics should be matched across seams (see PATTERNED FABRICS).

PATTERNED FABRICS   217

ABOVE *A pelmet can be used to alter the proportions of a window.*

BOX PELMET

Pelmets give a decorative and formal finish to the tops of curtains. A fabric pelmet consists of three layers: a top fabric and lining which are bonded to an adhesive-coated stiffener and then slipstitched together around the edges. The pelmet is fixed to a support board over the window with touch and close spots or tacks. Use tacks with decorative heads or hide the ordinary type and emphasize the pelmet edge with braid. The box pelmet is the easiest to make as no pattern needed.

Cutting out the pelmet
Measure for the pelmet (see MEASURING UP) and cut the top fabric to the correct size, adding 1.5cm (⅝in) for turnings to all edges. Pin, tack and stitch widths together if necessary to gain the correct length.

From the lining fabric cut out one piece the same size as the top. Next cut a piece of pelmet stiffener to the correct size, but do not include allowances for turnings.

Assembling the pelmet
Press the top fabric strip and lay it flat with the wrong side uppermost. Peel off the backing from one side of the stiffener and position centrally over the fabric. Press down and smooth in place. Peel the backing from the upper side of the stiffener, then fold over the edges of the top fabric and press in place (**1**).

Iron the lining smooth and press 1.5cm (⅝in) to the wrong side all round. Place the lining over the stiffener, matching outer edges, and carefully press down and smooth in place. Pin the edges of the lining to the top fabric and slipstitch together. Fold in 10cm (4in) at each end of the pelmet strip and crease well for the side sections (**2**).

If the pelmet is to be untrimmed fasten it to the board with touch and close spots. Stitch the touch and close spots to the wrong side of the pelmet 8cm (3in) apart. Stick the opposite halves of the spots to the pelmet board to correspond.

Alternatively, tack in place and trim.

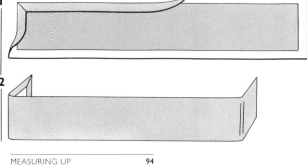

SHAPED PELMET

A pelmet does not have to be mounted on a board, it can be attached to the walls either side of a window recess as illustrated. A pattern is cut from dressmaker's pattern paper for the decorative edge of this pelmet and it is made up following the Box Pelmet instructions. Touch and close spots are then sewn on to the pelmet back and the corresponding halves stuck to the wall.

Making the pelmet
Measure the width of the recess and add 13cm (5in) to this measurement. Decide on the depth of the pelmet at the deepest and narrowest points.

If you do not want to use metric pattern paper for the pattern, rule your own in inches using plain paper, a yardstick and a set square.

Draw in the sides of the pelmet on the paper at the correct distance apart. Locate the narrowest points of the pelmet and the points of the curves at correctly proportioned intervals in between. Then join these points, using a flexible curve or the rim of a plate or other round object as a guide (**1**). Cut out the pattern.

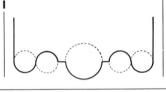

Using the pattern, cut one piece of lining, stiffener and top fabric, allowing 1.5cm ($\frac{5}{8}$in) for turnings all round the lining and top fabric pieces. Complete the pelmet as before (see BOX PELMET).

SOME PELMET IDEAS

Flat and box pelmets can have a variety of decoratively shaped edges. The shape can pick up a decorative theme in the room, be cut to suit the style of the curtains if it is a box pelmet, or add a touch of drama to an otherwise plain room.

Certain fabrics suit particular pelmet designs better than others.

Stripes go with castellations and florals with curvy shapes. You can even satin stitch round a floral design and then cut away the excess fabric to form a decorative edge.

The flat surface of a pelmet is an ideal surface for appliqué. Cutwork also looks pretty, as light shines through the design.

ABOVE *Soften the lines of a
deep recess with a
decoratively edged pelmet.*

SWAGS AND TAILS

Swags and tails look best against long windows set in a room with a high ceiling. Match the fabric to that of the curtains, but highlight the edges with narrow double frills and contrasting velvet ribbon. Both swags and tails need to be lined to give the folds a rounded feel. The swags are cut on the cross.

Making the swags

Fix a pelmet board of the desired width above the window (see MEASURING UP). The front edge of the board will equal the short back edge of each swag. The long front edge should equal the length of the desired amount of drape. Use a tape measure or a length of string to gauge this length (**1**).

The side edges of each swag should measure about one sixth of the curtain length after pleating up into 5cm to 10cm (2in–4in) wide knife pleats (see PLEATS). Cut out one piece of fabric on the cross to this size, allowing 1.5cm (⅝in) all round for seams. Cut out one piece of lining to the same size.

For the frill measure the base edge and make up a double 8cm (3in) wide frill to twice this measurement (see FRILLS). With raw edges even, pin and tack the frill to the right side of the swag base. With right sides together and raw edges even, pin, tack and stitch the lining and top

fabric together, leaving the top edge of the swag open (**2**). Trim and turn to the right side.

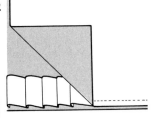

Turn down both top edges to the wrong side for 1.5cm (⅝in). Position a length of touch and close fastening along the raw edges (**3**). Pin, tack and stitch in place. Stick the opposite half of the fastening to the pelmet board.

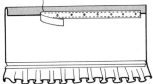

Pleat the swag at each side, beginning about 10cm (4in) from the top edge. Pin and tack. Hand stitch the pleats from the back at each side. If necessary, catch the pleats invisibly together at equally spaced intervals across the swag.

Position velvet ribbon to the right side of the swag centrally over the frill seamline (**4**). Pin, tack and stitch in place.

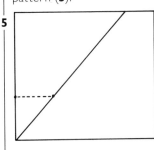

Making the tails

For each tail make up a piece of fabric 130cm long by 180cm wide (51in by 71in), plus 1.5cm seam allowance all round. Repeat for the lining. Next make a paper pattern for the base edge of the tail. Cut a piece of paper 90cm (36in) square. At the left-hand corner measure up from the edge for 30cm (12in) and mark. Measure in for 30cm (12in) and mark. Rule a line from the left-hand corner to this mark, continuing the line to the opposite edge. Cut along the line. The triangular shape is the pattern (**5**).

5

Fold the fabric in half lengthways. Place the shortest edge of the pattern against the fabric

fold with the pattern corner 1.5cm (⅝in) from the base edge of the fabric. Mark and cut along the diagonal edge of the pattern, allowing 1.5cm (⅝in) for the seam. Repeat for the lining.

Make up a double frill in the same way as for the swag and with raw edges even, pin and tack to the right side of the tail along the base edge.

Place the lining against the right side of the fabric with raw edges even. Pin, tack and stitch all round, leaving the top edge open. Trim and turn to the right side.

Pin and stitch velvet ribbon along the seamline as for the swag. Turn the top raw edges of the fabric and lining inwards for 1.5cm (⅝in) and slipstitch the opening together.

Measure in 30cm (12in) from each long side edge and fold the fabric to the centre from this point. Pin and tack across the top edges of the tail to hold the pleat in position and, if necessary, hand stitch together at the centre.

Fix each tail in place over the swags with touch and close fastening or hand stitching.

At the side edges make up half a tail, allowing sufficient fabric to cover the return at the side of the pelmet.

ABOVE *This type of window treatment looks best against tall windows in a room with elegant rather than homely furniture.*

SIX TIE-BACKS

Filled tie-back
First measure round the curtain to obtain the length of the tie-back. Hold a tape measure loosely round the curtain at the height you want the tie-back. To this measurement add a 3cm

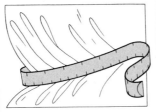

($1\frac{1}{4}$in) allowance for seams. Decide on the tie-back width and cut out one piece of fabric that measures twice the width plus 3cm ($1\frac{1}{4}$in).

Fold the fabric in half lengthways with right sides together. Pin, tack and stitch. Press the seam over the centre and then pin, tack and stitch across the ends, leaving a central opening in one of them. Trim and turn to the right side.

Cut a length of heavyweight wadding to fit

inside the tie-back. Insert the wadding and turn in the opening edges in line with the remainder of the seam. Slipstitch together to close.

Blanket stitch a curtain ring centrally to the underside of each end, so that the rings just overlap the ends.

Make up a second tie-back in the same way.

Plaited tie-back
Measure round the curtain to obtain the tie-back length as explained in the filled tie-back instructions.

Decide on the width of the tie-back and divide this measurement by three. Make up three differently coloured tubes that will measure the correct size when plaited. Follow the instructions for the filled tie-back, but use mediumweight wadding for the filling.

Place the three tubes

side by side, overlapping one set of ends, and carefully hand stitch together. Plait the lengths. At the opposite end, hand stitch the lengths together as before.

Blanket stitch a curtain ring centrally to the underside of each end.

Make up a second tie-back in the same way.

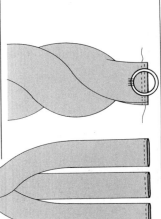

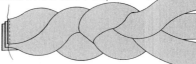

Bow-trimmed tie-back
Measure round the curtain to obtain the tie-back length as explained in the filled tie-back instructions. Decide on the tie-back width.

Make up a plain straight tie-back as follows. Cut two pieces of fabric to size, allowing 1.5cm ($\frac{5}{8}$in) for seams. Cut out two pieces of iron-on interfacing to size, omitting the seam allowance. Position the interfacing centrally to the wrong side of one fabric piece and press in place. Place the tie-back pieces

with right sides together and pin, tack and stitch all round, leaving a central opening in one side. Trim and turn to the right side. Turn in the opening edges in line with the remainder of the seam and slipstitch to close.

Stitch a ring to each end in the same way as for the filled tie-back.

For the bow cut two pieces of fabric 93cm by 11cm ($36\frac{1}{2}$in by $4\frac{1}{2}$in). Place with right sides together; pin, tack and stitch together all round, leaving an opening in one side.

Trim and turn to the right side. Turn in the opening edges with the remainder of the seam and slipstitch.

For the centre loop cut one piece of fabric 11cm ($4\frac{1}{4}$in) square. Fold in half with right sides together; pin, tack and stitch the long edges. Trim and turn to the right side. Press the seam to the centre.

Fold the bow length into a bow and pin. Fold the loop over the centre of the bow, turn in the raw edges and slipstitch together. Hand stitch the bow to the tie-back.

INTERFACINGS 196   STITCHES 197   STITCHES 197

V-shaped tie-back

Measure round the curtain to obtain the tie-back length as explained in the filled tie-back instructions. On a piece of paper mark a rectangle that measures half the length by 28cm (11in). Measure 14cm (5½in) up from the bottom left-hand corner and rule a line from this point to the right-hand corner. Then measure 5cm (2in) down from this corner and rule a diagonal line to the bottom left-hand corner from this point.

Striped tie-back

Measure round the curtain to obtain the tie-back length as explained in the filled tie-back instructions. Decide on the width and divide this into three equal sections, adding a 3cm (1¼in) allowance for seams to each piece. Cut out each piece from a different fabric.

For the back cut out one piece to the complete tie-back size, including a 1.5cm (⅝in) seam allowance on all sides. Join the three

Piped shaped tie-back

Measure round the curtain to obtain the tie-back length as explained in the filled tie-back instructions.

On a sheet of paper mark a strip about 11cm (4½in) wide by half the length measurement. Gently curve both sides of the strip so one end is narrowed down to about 4cm (1½in). Cut out the pattern.

Fold the fabric in half. Place the wide end of the pattern against the fabric fold and cut out, adding a 1.5cm (⅝in) seam

Fold the fabric in half. Place the wide end of the pattern against the fabric fold and cut out, adding a 1.5cm (⅝in) seam allowance. Cut out the other side of the tie-back in the same way and then cut one piece from lightweight wadding.

Place the wadding to the wrong side of one fabric piece; pin and tack. Make lines of quilting stitches both ways across the wrong side of the tie-back piece to form 3cm (1¼in) squares, using embroidery cotton

strips together, taking a 1.5cm (⅝in) seam allowance to form the tie-back front.

From heavyweight iron-on interfacing cut out one piece to the complete tie-back size, omitting the seam allowance. Position the interfacing centrally over the wrong side of the back piece and press.

Place the tie-back pieces with right sides together and pin, tack and stitch all round alongside the interfacing edge, leaving an opening at one end.

allowance. Repeat to cut out the other side of the tie-back. Then cut out one piece from heavyweight iron-on interfacing, omitting the seam allowance and apply to the wrong side of the tie-back.

Measure around the tie-back pattern. Make up a 4cm (1½in) wide bias strip to this length plus 2cm (¾in) and cover the cord (see PIPING). Attach the piping to one tie-back piece.

With right sides together and raw edges even, pin, tack and stitch

on the bobbin.

Place the tie-back pieces with right sides together and raw edges even. Pin, tack and stitch all round, leaving an opening for turning. Trim and turn to the right side. Turn in the opening edges in line with the remainder of the seam and slipstitch together.

Blanket stitch a curtain ring to each end as explained in the filled tie-back instructions.

Make up a second tie-back in the same way.

Trim the seams and turn to the right side. Turn in the opening edges in line with the remainder of the seam and slipstitch to close.

Blanket stitch a curtain ring to each end as explained in the filled tie-back instructions.

Make up a second tie-back in the same way.

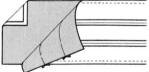

the tie-back pieces together all round, leaving an opening at one side. Trim and turn to right

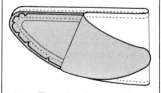

side. Turn in the opening edges and slipstitch.

Blanket stitch a curtain ring to each end as explained in the filled tie-back instructions.

Make up a second tie-back in the same way.

MEASURING UP – BLINDS

Roller blinds

On windows with a deep recess it is usual to position the blind against the glazed area of the window. Use an expandable metal rule to measure horizontally from one side of the recess to the other. Deduct 1.5cm ($\frac{5}{8}$in) at each side for the pin end and spring mechanism. Position the brackets about 3cm (1$\frac{1}{4}$in) from the top of the recess to allow for the full roller. Measure the drop of the blind from the top of the roller.

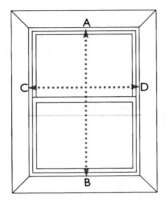

On windows with no recess the blind is mounted on the window frame if there is a suitable flat piece and, if not, on the wall beyond the frame. More light will be excluded if the blind extends behind the top and sides of the window.

Roman blinds

Roman blinds are fixed at the window on a length of 50mm by 25mm (2in by 1in) battening. In a window recess the batten will be fitted to the ceiling of the recess. On these windows measure the drop of the blind from the top of the batten to the sill. For the width measure the length of the batten.

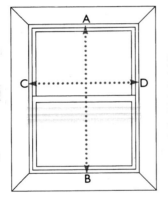

On a window without a recess, the batten will have to be mounted on supports. In this case, position the supports above the window at the desired height. Measure the window as before.

Austrian blinds

Austrian blinds are gathered at the top by heading tape and they hang at the window on a special track fitted with eyelets. Mount the track inside the window recess in the usual way and calculate the width of fabric needed by multiplying the fullness required for the heading tape by the track width (see HEADINGS).

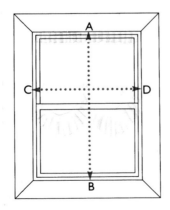

On a window without a recess the track should extend 15cm (6in) beyond the edges of a plain window and should be flush with the edges of a molded window frame. The drop should be measured from the top of the track to the sill.

HEADINGS, TRACKS AND POLES   206

ABOVE *An awkwardly shaped window has been successfully covered with a roller blind.*

ROLLER BLIND

The clean unobtrusive lines of the roller blind look right in any setting. A blind kit supplies all the components needed to make one up: a wooden roller, brackets, a cord pull and a narrow lath that is slotted through the blind base to help it hang well.

This blind has been made from specially stiffened fabric that means the sides do not have to be hemmed. It is held in place against the glass with a wooden curtain rod.

Making the blind

Cut the roller to size if necessary and then fix the brackets and roller in place. Measure the width of the roller and the length of the window. Cut one piece of stiffened fabric to this size, adding 30cm (2in) to the length to allow for the casing and to make sure the roller is still covered when the blind is fully extended. At the base edge fold under a double 4cm (1½in) hem to the wrong side. Press and stitch across the hem and down one side to make a casing. Trim the lath to fit the casing minus 2cm (¾in). Insert the lath (**1**) and stitch across the open end of the casing.

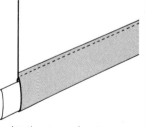

At the top edge turn down 1.5cm (⅝in) to the right side and finger press. With the blind right side up, lay the roller across the blind with the spring mechanism to the left. Place the top folded edge along the marked guideline on the roller. Hammer tacks in place at 2cm (¾in) intervals (**2**) with one at each end.

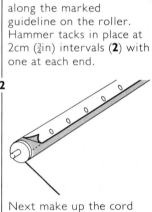

Next make up the cord pull. Thread one end of the cord through the holder and knot, then thread the opposite end through the acorn. Screw the cord holder centrally to the lath on the right side of the blind (**3**).

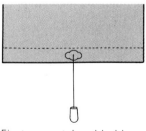

Fix two metal rod holders on either side of the window where it slopes. Cut a length of rod to fit and slot in place. Hang the blind in the brackets and run it down behind the rod.

AUSTRIAN BLIND

Austrian blinds provide the frilly window covering that can soften an otherwise plain room. And, using a special Austrian blind track, fixing the blind in place is as easy as hanging a pair of curtains. The blind is drawn up in the same way as the Roman blind, with cords running through rows of narrow looped tape stitched to the back. To give the blind a really full look a lining can be added.

Making the blind
Fix the Austrian blind track in position at the window (see HEADINGS, TRACKS AND POLES). Measure the window (see MEASURING UP) and make up one piece of fabric to twice the width measurement by the drop plus 45cm (18in).

Fold under a double 1cm (⅜in) turning on both side edges of the blind; pin, tack and stitch in place.

On the wrong side of the blind, mark the positions of the outer rows of looped tape 10cm (4in) from the hemmed edges. Pin, tack and stitch in place, making sure the loops match horizontally across the blind (**1**), and with the first row of loops 3cm (1¼in) up from base edge. Position the

remaining rows of tape in between at about 30cm (12in) intervals; pin, tack and stitch.

For optional frill, cut a 16cm (6½in) wide strip of fabric to equal twice the width of the blind. Stitch strips together if necessary, with narrow French seams, to gain the correct width.

Turn under a double 1cm (⅜in) hem along the side and base edges of the frill strip, mitring the corners (see FOLDING MITRED CORNERS). Pin, tack and stitch in place.

Work two rows of gathering stitches along the top edge of the frill, dividing the gathering into sections if the frill is very long.

With right sides together, place the frill to the blind base edge and pull up the gathers evenly to fit. Pin, tack and stitch the frill in place, catching in the tape edges and taking a 2cm (¾in) seam

allowance on the blind base and 1.5cm (⅝in) on the frill (**2**). Trim down the frill seam allowance. Turn under the raw edge of the blind seam allowance and place flat against the blind; stitch in place to neaten.

Turn down the top edge of the blind by 1cm (⅜in). Attach heading tape to the top edge of the blind (see HEADINGS, TRACKS AND POLES). Fit the gathered tape with curtain hooks and hang the blind.

Threading the track
Fix a cleat to the right-hand side of the window. On the opposite side,

begin threading the cords; each length should be twice the blind length plus one width. Knot a cord to the bottom loop on the first row of tape. Then take the cord up through all the loops on that row of tape and then to the right through the eyes along the track.

Repeat with each row of tape, until all the cords are hanging together at the cleat side of the window. Knot the cords together and trim the ends level with the window sill. Pull up the blind and wind the cords tightly around the cleat (**3**).

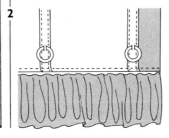

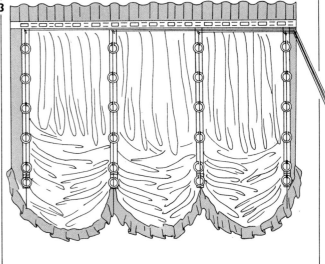

ABOVE *Austrian blinds have the dual advantage of looking like curtains when let down, but not cluttering the window when pulled up.*

ROMAN BLIND

Stylish and tailored, Roman blinds pull up into even folds across a window by means of cords slotted through ringed tape that is stitched to the back of the blind. The cords are knotted together and secured round a cleat positioned at the side of the window.

There is a variety of tapes on the market with rings or loops fixed at regular intervals. Fabric widths should be joined together with plain flat seams evenly placed across the blind. The blind is lined to ensure that it hangs well. Choose a good quality cotton sateen for the lining.

Cutting out the fabrics

Measure the window (see MEASURING UP). Fix the appropriate length of 50mm by 25mm (2in by 1in) battening temporarily in place.

To work out the width of the blind add 9cm (3½in) for side turnings to the batten length. For the length, measure from the top of the batten to the sill, adding 15cm (6in) for the hem casing and the amount of fabric needed to fix the blind to the batten. Cut out or make up a piece of fabric to this size.

For the lining make up or cut a piece the same length but 3cm (1¼in) less in width than the batten.

Attaching the lining

Mark the centres of both fabric pieces at the top and bottom of the blind.

With right sides together, pin, tack and stitch the top fabric to the lining along the side edges, taking a 1.5cm (⅝in) seam allowance. Press the seams open and turn the blind to the right side.

With the lined side facing, pin the fabric centres together at the top and bottom and press the pieces flat so a margin of top fabric is formed down each side edge of the blind (**1**).

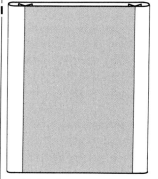

At the bottom edge, working with both fabrics together, turn 1cm (⅜in) and then 10cm (4in) to the wrong side to form the hem; pin in place.

Attaching the tape, lath and screw eyes

Pin lengths of ringed tape, each as long as the blind, to the lined side. Begin by covering each seamline, making sure that the rings match up horizontally and with the first row of rings just above hem edge. Tuck the raw ends inside the hem. Position more rows in between at 25cm to 40cm (10in–16in) intervals. Using a zipper foot, stitch the rows of tape down each side through both layers of fabric.

Stitch across the hem edge, catching in ends of tape. Stitch across the hem again 4cm (1½in) below the first row of stitching to form a casing for the lath. This should equal the length of the casing minus 2cm (¾in). Insert the lath into the casing and slipstitch up both side edges to hold it firmly in place (**2**).

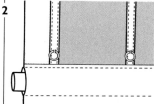

Next zigzag the two fabrics together along the top edge. Remove the batten from the window. Place the top edge of fabric over the top edge of the batten and tack or staple in place. Position a screw eye into the underside of the batten above each row of ringed tape.

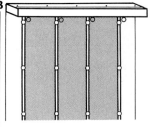

Threading the cords

Cut the cord into as many lengths as there are rows of tape. Each length should measure twice the length of the finished blind plus one width. Knot the first length to the bottom ring at the left-hand side. Thread the cord up through all the rings on the first tape and then through all the screw eyes to the right (**3**). Knot another cord to the first ring of the next row and repeat. Continue until all the cords are hanging together at the right-hand side. Replace the batten at the window.

Fix a cleat at the right-hand side of the window. Knot the cords together level with the sill; pull up the blind and wind the ends tightly around the cleat.

ABOVE *Choose fabric for a Roman blind that looks as good pleated up as in a straight length.*

108

ABOVE *The twisted shape of this window hanging adds a sculptural dimension to the room.*

TWISTED PULL-UP BLIND

This elegant hanging half covers the window and the filmy fabric filters the light. A narrow cord slotted through a central casing pulls the hanging into the unusual twisted shape. The fabric and cord are attached to a batten fixed at the top of the window.

Making the blind

Measure the window (see MEASURING UP) and cut a 50mm by 25mm (2in by 1in) batten to fit.

For the blind width, add 2.5cm (1in) for side turnings to the width of the batten. For the length, measure from the top of the batten to the sill. Add 5cm (2in) for the hem and the amount of fabric needed to fix the blind to the batten, and 20cm (8in) for the twist take-up. Cut out one piece of fabric to this size. Turn under a double 6mm ($\frac{1}{4}$in) hem along the side edges and base, mitring the corners (see FOLDING MITRED CORNERS); pin in place.

Mark the centre of the blind lengthways with a row of pins. Pin a length of 1cm ($\frac{3}{8}$in) wide tape to the wrong side of the blind centrally over the row of pins, removing the pins as you position the tape (**1**).

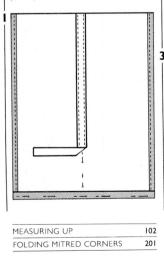

Tack and stitch the tape in place down both long edges. Thread one blind length of narrow, soft cord down the centre of the tape and pin to hold at the top. Tuck both tape and cord ends inside the hem. Stitch the side and base hems (**2**).

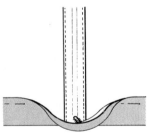

Position the top of the fabric over the batten and staple or tack in place. Hold the batten in position at the window top. Pull up the cord to create the twisted effect and until the bottom corners of the blind are just touching the sill. Cut off the excess cord and staple to the batten. Fix the batten in place.

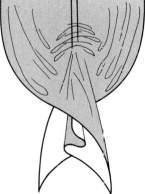

SHEER BLIND IDEAS

Take a length of gauze or other loosely woven cloth and transform a plain window into a sculptural focal point. Each of these ideas is easy to accomplish using tapes and casings. Most elegant of all is the sail – simply fix the curtain at all four corners using screw-in hooks and eyelets. To draw, just pull up one corner with a length of cord.

SIX BLINDS

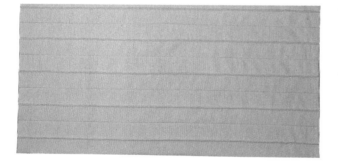

Shaped roller blind
Make a pattern for the base edge as follows. Cut a rectangle of paper, the length equal to the finished width of the blind, and fold in half. Working freehand, shape the base edge into a curve. Cut out the pattern.

Cut out one piece of top fabric and lining to the desired size (see MEASURING UP) plus 3cm (1¼in) seam allowance. Place the lining and top fabric with right sides together; position the pattern along the base edge and mark round. Taking a 1.5cm seam allowance, pin, tack and stitch the blind pieces together, leaving 4cm (1½in) openings in each side, just above shaped edge. Trim and turn. Stitch across the blind in line with the top and bottom edges of the openings to form the casing. Finish the blind.

Tucked Roman blind
Cut one piece of top fabric and one of lining to the desired width and length (see ROMAN BLIND), adding 3cm (1¼in) to the width for seams and 13cm (6in) to the length for the casing and fixing, plus 12mm (½in) for each tuck.

Spacing the tucks evenly, mark tuck positions across the blind. Join the top fabric and lining and make the bottom casing (see ROMAN BLIND).

Fold the fabric on the marked lines, stitching across each row 6mm (¼in) from the foldline and alternating the rows on the outside and inside of the blind. Stitch curtain rings at 30cm (12in) intervals across the inward facing tucks, placing the outer rings 2cm (¾in) from the edges. Attach to the batten and thread with cords.

Festoon blind
Cut one piece of fabric to the desired length and width (see MEASURING UP, Austrian blind), allowing 1.5cm (⅝in) for seams and subtracting 10cm (4in) from the length.

Make up a 9.5cm (3¾in) wide strip of fabric that measures twice the length of the side and base edges. Turn under a double 1cm (⅜in) hem along one edge. Make up a 12.5cm (5in) wide strip and hem as before. Place the strips one on top of the other and work two rows of gathering 1.5cm (⅝in) from the raw edges.

Attach looped tape to the blind, the first lengths about 3cm (1¼in) away from the raw side edges, the first horizontal row of loops 3cm (1¼in) up from the base edge.

With right sides together and raw edges even, stitch the double frill to the right side of the blind, pulling up the gathers evenly to fit.

ROMAN BLIND   106
MEASURING UP   102
MEASURING UP   102

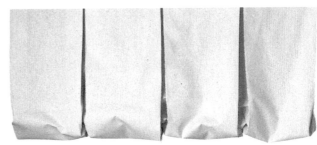

Cutwork roller blind

To make the pattern for the cutwork shape cut out a rectangle of paper 4cm by 2cm (1½in by ¾in). Cut one piece of top fabric and one of lining to desired size of the blind (see MEASURING UP), adding 3cm (1¼in) to the width and 5cm (2in) to the length. Place the top fabric and lining with right sides together; pin, tack and stitch down the sides. Trim and turn.

Working with both fabrics together, mark the centre of the blind and a line 12cm (5in) up from base edge. Using the pattern, mark six evenly spaced rectangles along the marked line at a 45 degree angle, ranging either side of the blind centre. Zigzag stitch round each shape just inside the marked edges to form a satin stitch effect. Discard the centre fabric.

Bordered Roman blind

Cut one piece of top fabric and one of lining to the desired size (see MEASURING UP), allowing 3cm (1¼in) for seams on the width minus 10cm (4in) for the border and 8cm (3in) on the length for the bottom seam and fixing, minus 5cm (2in) for the border.

From the contrast fabric cut two strips 13cm (5¼in) wide to equal the length of the blind plus 6.5cm (2⅝in), and one strip to equal the width plus 6.5cm (2⅝in). Fold each strip in half lengthways and press. Make up the border, leaving the seams unstitched for 1.5cm (⅝in) at either end (see CO-ORDINATED TABLECLOTHS).

With right sides together and raw edges even, stitch the border to the right side of the blind along one inner edge. Attach ringed tape to the blind. Turn under the border and hem.

Pleated blind

Cut one piece of top fabric and one of lining to the desired length (see ROMAN BLIND) plus 1.5cm (⅝in) seam allowance. For the width allow for 15cm (6in) inverted pleats spaced between 24cm and 32cm (9½in–12½in) apart. Follow the line sequence given for inverted box pleats (see PLEATS).

Place the fabric and lining with right sides together; pin tack and stitch the side seams. Trim and turn. Mark in the placement and pleat lines at the top and bottom of the blind. Pleat up. Stitch across the blind at the top and bottom.

Turn up the base edge and stitch a length of 5cm (2in) wide tape across the base. Stitch rows of curtain rings to the centre back of the pleats, with the first row positioned along the casing and then at 20cm (8in) intervals up the blind. Tie the bottom two rings together.

CHAIRS
AND
CUSHIONS

We choose different styles of seating to sit on and to support our bodies according to whether we are working, eating or relaxing. The chair or sofa may be padded or we will make it more comfortable with cushions. Fabric coverings for seats and cushions offer masses of decorative possibilities. Keep in mind the practical treatment the seat is to receive and where it is to go, and then let your imagination have full rein.

Upholstered armchairs and sofas are often fitted with intricate loose covers that are tailor made to their shape rather in the way that a suit is cut and sewn. To carry the clothing analogy further, there are many more ways of dressing a chair than in the basic tailored box or frilly flounced skirt. Just as with clothes, dressing a chair is a question of overall style and a sense of line, plus attention to finer detail.

The simplest way to cover a chair, however – the furnishing equivalent of wearing a toga – is to throw or drape something over it. Quilts and Paisley shawls make excellent throws. If you are using a piece of furnishing fabric be generous with the amount for this casual look to appear really stylish. This is also an excellent way of testing a proposed fabric. Leave it there for a few days to see how it works with the rest of the room. Shops will sometimes lend swatches of fabric so you don't have to spend money on your experimental throw. Take this idea a stage further: instead of just throwing large pieces of fabric over the furniture, knot them in position, securing them around the legs. Use differently coloured pieces of fabric.

RIGHT *Chairs with exposed wooden frames can easily be covered with loose covers. These form calm oases of colour in a large empty room.*

At the other extreme is the couture approach to covering upholstered furniture. Gianfranco Ferre, the Italian couturier, made three outfits for a sofa and an armchair. Each was tailor made with kick pleats, and the softly draped backs were fastened with a long row of pearl buttons in place of a zip fastener. One dress was for summer days in linen with drawn threadwork detailing, the second was for winter in thick warm wool with rug tassel trimmings, and the third, the evening dress, was in jewel-coloured taffeta. He made it a condition of sale that two outfits had to be bought with each item of furniture.

BELOW and RIGHT *The two extremes in loose covers – one that involves maximum fitting and the other a simple 'throw'.*

Although making up sets of loose covers to suit the season or occasion would be extravagant in the extreme, the idea is worth imitating. Cushions could be given different coverings for different times of the year, or they could be dressed up for a special occasion. Taffeta would be very impractical for a chair cover, but a cushion covered with silk taffeta with the opening closed with pearl buttons would look charming.

If you do choose clothing fabric for soft furnishings, be sure that it will be able to stand up to the wear and tear it will receive. For a

loose cover with a frilled skirt, tough denim fabric makes an amusing and surprising contrast with the feminine frill. This chair could also button down the back as did Gianfranco Ferre's – choose brightly coloured buttons, and it could look good in a child's room.

Home in on such details on any loose covers. Take the kick pleats on a sofa or chair right up to the seat, or make bold wide box pleats all the way round the sofa at this height. Piping is attached to sofas to strengthen edges as well as for decoration. Instead of just the same or a contrasting colour, make piping up in a checked or striped fabric. Cut into the fabric along the hemline and shape it into scallops, points or castellations. If the fabric is patterned and the design lends itself to this, cut around motifs to give an outlined shape to

LEFT Grey linen makes an unusual covering for an antique chair, the matt fabric a subtle contrast with the shiny gilt.

LEFT A rigid molded seat gives shape to a quilted covering. This is a good disguise for any hard and unattractive seating that cannot be disposed of.

Even the most ordinary piece of furniture can be transformed by dressing it up.

BELOW *Bright colours hold
their own in sunlight. These
striped loungers have a
cheerful 'seaside' feel.*

the hem. Kick pleat insets can be in different colours or fabrics.

Chaises longues are often covered in velvet or Regency stripes, but they also look wonderful in bright solid colours, in humble mattress ticking or wide oriental stripes, in wool tartan or plain cream calico. Cover a chaise longue in a small flower-sprigged pattern with a border print to frame the contours; finish with a bolster and a neatly folded rug so that it becomes a day bed.

Those small armless chairs (the type often seen in waiting-rooms) can look terrific when dressed in long skirted covers that hide their twiggy legs and convert them into pretty seats as well as something comfortable to sit on. Even the discarded bucket seat from an old car will flourish under this treatment. If floral prints are used, make them outsize with the main flower placed in a central position on each seat. Cane sofas and seats can be made to look luxurious as well as comfortable with the

addition of the type of boxed cushions often found on sofas and armchairs.

Dining and kitchen chairs usually have wooden backs, with wooden, cane or upholstered seats. To start with the wooden-seated variety, the rustic type found in the kitchen, little squab cushions that are tied to the back work well on these seats as they do not slither around. Make them from thinly stuffed patchwork or make mats of plaited rags or small tufted mattresses in bright colours. If young children use the kitchen, stitch a set of easily washable covers and then exchange these with other sets for evenings and parties. A slip cover can be made for the back of these chairs. Make it from quilted fabric to give softness. If you have bench seating, cover the bench with box cushions and make up basic square cushions for backrests. Attach a length of battening to the wall and insert cup hooks, then stitch loops to the cushions and slip them over the hooks.

Dining chairs, even the upholstered ones, can be enveloped with loose covers; indeed this was quite common in previous times, when precious upholstery needed to be protected. Use square, tailored shapes for rectangular chairs and covers with flouncy valances for curvilinear shapes.

Why not solve a storage problem and make winter coverings for garden furniture so it can be used indoors in cold weather. Cover lounging mattresses with quilted fabric, replace the canvas of deck and director's chairs with velvet or suede and give the cushions of wicker chairs new warmly coloured covers.

Cushions have been referred to so far as adjuncts of chairs, but it is surprising how quickly a room can be brightened up just with the addition of new cushion covers. They can make marvellous splashes of colour grouped together on a sofa or bed, in different shapes and sizes, maybe echoing the colours of a picture above. Silly frilly cushions that carry intimate or amusing messages in appliqué or embroidery are good for conversation.

Tiers of firmly stuffed cushions, stacked

ABOVE *Cushions and mattresses in tough cotton canvas make adaptable outdoor furniture that looks casual and relaxing.*

three or four high, secured together and trimmed with rope make good occasional seats. Firmly stuffed cubes also make good seats or tables for children, each side a different colour or pattern for a patchwork effect.

Any type of fabric can be used for a cushion. Precious lace can be backed with a coloured or plain fabric. Expensive fabric such as crewel embroidery, or small scraps of kelim rug can be made into cushions and backed with plain fabric. Lurex, velvet and tweed, and tartan and other dress fabrics can all be used. The expense of covering cushions is minimal compared to other soft furnishing projects, the effects are great and the choice endless. So why not begin with one first?

BELOW A floral and linear decorative theme has been united by the choice of colour and a white background. Masses of cushions look luxurious but cost relatively little to cover.

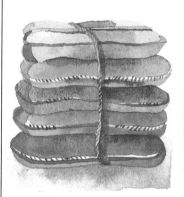

Stack up cushions and secure with rope or cord for a comfortable seat.

ABOVE *Cushions and boisters can make comfortable back- and armrests in any type of unpadded chair.*

121

CHAIR COVER IDEAS

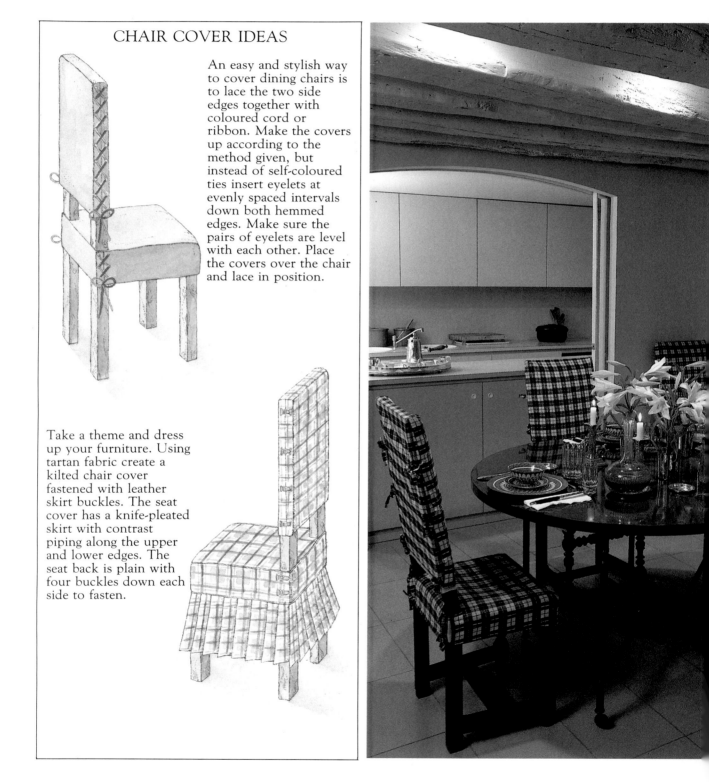

An easy and stylish way to cover dining chairs is to lace the two side edges together with coloured cord or ribbon. Make the covers up according to the method given, but instead of self-coloured ties insert eyelets at evenly spaced intervals down both hemmed edges. Make sure the pairs of eyelets are level with each other. Place the covers over the chair and lace in position.

Take a theme and dress up your furniture. Using tartan fabric create a kilted chair cover fastened with leather skirt buckles. The seat cover has a knife-pleated skirt with contrast piping along the upper and lower edges. The seat back is plain with four buckles down each side to fasten.

TIE-ON DINING CHAIR COVERS

This is one of the easiest ways to cover chairs. The backs of the dining chairs are oblongs of fabric seamed together at the top of each chair. Each seat is covered with a square of fabric split at the back corners.

Making the seat cover
Measure the seat both ways including the side sections. Add 2cm ($\frac{3}{4}$in) seam allowance all round. Cut out a piece of fabric to these dimensions.

Place the fabric, wrong side up, centrally over the seat. Pin the excess fabric at the front corners into darts (**1**). Remove the cover and stitch the front darts; trim and press open.

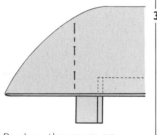

Replace the cover on the seat with the right side up. Cut up the fabric at the back strut positions and then cut out a square of fabric for each leg, leaving a 1cm ($\frac{3}{8}$in) allowance on all sides (**2**). Turn under a double 6mm ($\frac{1}{4}$in) hem around the square and opening pin, tack and stitch.

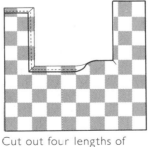

Cut out four lengths of 30cm by 3cm (12in by 1$\frac{1}{4}$in) of

self-fabric for the ties. Fold each piece of fabric in half lengthways. Tuck under 6mm ($\frac{1}{4}$in) along the long edges and at one end. Pin, tack and topstitch the tucked-in edges; press.

Position a pair of ties at each back corner, turn in the raw edges and stitch them in place just under the cover edge (**3**). Zigzag the base edges. Turn in for 2cm ($\frac{3}{4}$in) and catch in place.

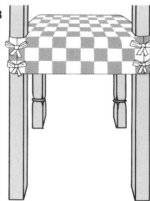

Making the back cover
Measure the height and width of the seat back. Add 1.5cm ($\frac{5}{8}$in) seam allowance to the top and 2cm ($\frac{3}{4}$in) to the side and base edges. Cut out a piece of fabric to this size.

Measure the height of the front, beginning at the top back edge of the seat and adding hem and seam allowances as before. Measure the width from the back edge of the chair back, round the front to the other back edge. Add 2cm ($\frac{3}{4}$in) to the side edges.

Cut one piece of fabric to this size. Join the back and front cover pieces at the top edges.

Place the cover wrong side up over the chair back

and pin the fabric together at the top corners (**4**). Remove the cover and stitch. Trim.

Turn under a double 1cm ($\frac{3}{8}$in) hem down the side edges; pin, tack and stitch down each hem. Zigzag stitch the raw base edges. Turn under for 2cm ($\frac{3}{4}$in) and catch in place.

Make up six pairs of self-fabric ties in the same way as for the seat cover, topstitching the seams

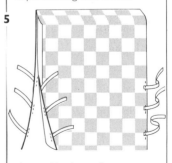

along all edges. Fasten to the outside of the cover at evenly spaced intervals down the side edges (**5**).

ABOVE *These seat and chair back covers brighten up a traditional set of dining-room chairs and are an easy project for a beginner.*

TIE-ON SOFA COVER

The rectangular sofa is covered in one piece of fabric, with self-fabric ties at the front and back corners and darts that eliminate the excess folds of fabric between the sofa sides and the backrest.

Making the sofa cover

For the length, measure from the base of the sofa back over the top of the sofa down the front and across the seat to the front base (**A-B**). Add 5cm (2in) to both edges for hems (**I**). For the width, measure from the base at one side, up the arm and down to the seat, across the seat and over the opposite arm, then down to the base again (**C-D**). Add hem allowances to each end as before. Cut a piece of fabric to these dimensions.

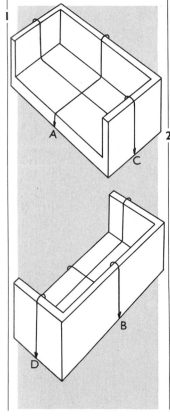

To gain the width, it will probably be necessary to join fabric widths together. If this is the case, position the seams evenly across the sofa. Take a 1.5cm ($\frac{5}{8}$in) seam allowance and sew plain flat seams.

Cut 12 strips of fabric 30cm by 2cm (12in by $\frac{3}{4}$in). Fold each tie in half lengthways with right sides together; pin, tack and stitch down the length and across one end, taking a 6mm ($\frac{1}{4}$in) seam allowance. Turn the tie to the right side.

Fitting the cover to the sofa

Place the fabric rectangle centrally over the sofa and mark the front openings down the outside front edges (**E-F**), following the lines of the upholstery (**I**).

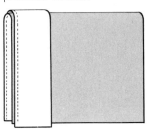

Mark the back openings down the outside back edges (**G-H**) in the same way. Cut up to the top of the marked positions. Tack the raw ends of three pairs of ties either side of each opening at evenly spaced intervals.

Cut a straight strip of fabric twice as long as one opening by 5.5cm (2$\frac{1}{4}$in) wide for the facing. Place the right side of the strip to the right side of the opening; pin, tack and stitch 3mm ($\frac{1}{8}$in) from the edge, only taking a few threads of fabric around the top of the opening (**3**). Press the raw edges on to the strip and then turn the strip to the wrong side of the cover. Turn under the remaining long raw edge of the strip for 3mm ($\frac{1}{8}$in) and slipstitch over the previous sitches.

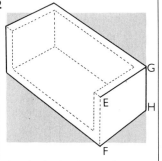

Repeat, to face each opening in the same way.

Replace the cover over the sofa and tie bows across the openings. Push the surplus fabric down around the seat. At the back corners fold up and pin the excess fabric into darts graduating down to the seat. Remove the cover; tack and stitch the corner darts. Trim off the excess fabric and neaten.

Turn under a double 2.5cm (1in) hem all round the outer edges of the cover. Pin, tack and stitch in place. Replace the cover over the sofa.

ABOVE *This type of cover is easy to put on and easy to remove for laundering — a plus point when using light-coloured fabric.*

TUB CHAIR COVER

These unusual covers pull over the tub chairs and tie underneath in a similar way to loose covers. They are very quick to assemble as they do not have to be fitted. The slight gathering at the top provides all the roominess that is needed.

Making the cover
Measure the length of the front arm gusset all round the chair from base to base, adding 15cm (6in) at each end for the base tuck-under (**1**). Then measure the width, adding 3cm (1¼in) to this measurement for seams. Cut a gusset strip to this size.

For the main cover, measure round the widest part of the chair back, from front gusset to front gusset. Add on 3cm (1¼in) for seams. Measure the height from gusset to base, adding 15cm (6in) for the base tuck-under plus a 1.5cm (⅝in) seam allowance. Cut out or make up a piece of fabric to this size.

Round off the top corners of the back cover, following the lines of the chair. Run a row of gathering stitches along the top edge of the back.

Place the back to the gusset, matching the base and front side edges. Pull up the gathering around the top edge to ease the back on to the gusset; pin, tack and stitch in place (**2**).

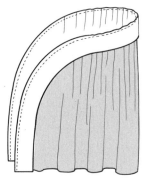

2

Next measure around the inside of the seat from gusset to gusset, adding 3cm (1¼in) for seams. Measure the height from the top of the inside front down to and across the seat and then down to the base. Add a 1.5cm (⅝in)

seam allowance and 15cm (6in) for tuck-under. Cut out or make up a piece of fabric to this size. Round off the front corners in the same way as the back. Run a row of gathering stitches along the inside front edge, as before.

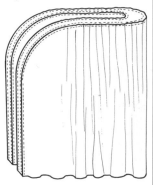

3

Place the inside front to the gusset, matching side and base edges. Pull up the gathering stitches along the top edge to ease the inside front in place. Pin, tack and stitch (**3**).

At the base edges turn under 4cm (1½in), then turn under a further 1cm (⅜in). Pin, tack and stitch close to the 1cm (⅜in) foldline to form a casing, leaving a gap in the stitching to provide an opening.

Thread a length of 1cm (⅜in) wide tape through the casing. Put the cover on the chair and pull up the ties to fit it around the base, spacing the gathers evenly. Tie the tapes and push the ends inside the cover.

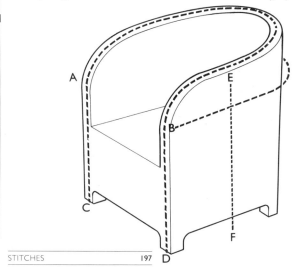

1

A B C D E F

ABOVE *Even the most unusually shaped chairs can be covered – just approach the problem as if you were fitting a dress.*

MEASURING UP – LOOSE COVERS

Make a rough sketch of your sofa as shown and mark on it the name of each section.

A outside back

B front (add tuck-in allowance to lower edge)

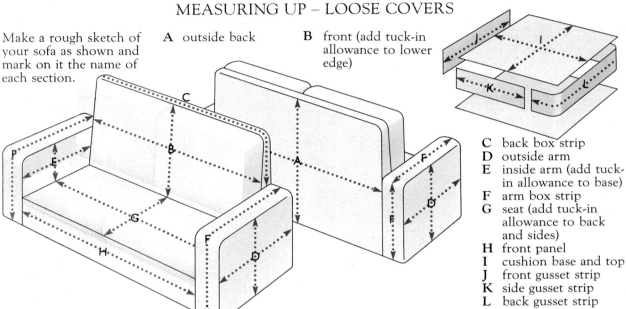

C back box strip
D outside arm
E inside arm (add tuck-in allowance to base)
F arm box strip
G seat (add tuck-in allowance to back and sides)
H front panel
I cushion base and top
J front gusset strip
K side gusset strip
L back gusset strip

Measure each section widthways and lengthways at the widest point. Write down the dimensions of each section on the drawing and indicate which way the straight grain of the fabric should run.

Decide on the style of skirt you want (see FRILLS AND PLEATS). For the skirt with inverted pleats illustrated on the opposite page, subtract 14cm (5½in) from the height of the outside back (**A**) and arms (**D**), the length of the arm box strip (**F**) and the depth of the front panel (**H**). Each skirt strip should correspond to a side of the sofa and be 18cm (7in) in depth. Allow 1.5cm (⅝in) at each strip end for joins. Three of the corner inserts measure 18cm (7in) square. The two

inserts that range either side of the back opening measure 18cm by 10cm (7in by 4in).

With the exception of the skirt and insert sections, add 5cm (2in) all round to your measurements to allow for seams and adjustment when pin fitting. Add 15cm (6in) for tuck-in and seams where indicated.

For each cushion measure the top of the cushion pad both ways and add 3cm (1¼in) seam allowance to these measurements. The gusset is divided into four pieces: front, sides, and a back piece which encloses a zip that extends around the back corners.

For the front gusset strip measure the length and width of the cushion front and add

3cm (1¼in) seam allowance to both measurements. For the back gusset strip measure the length of the cushion back and add 19cm (7½in); add 6cm (2½in) to the width to allow for the zip.

For the side gusset strips measure the length and width of one side and deduct 8cm (3in) from the length and add 3cm (1¼in) seam allowance to the width.

For the piping measure around the cushion top and double this measurement, allowing 10cm (4in) for joins. The zip should be 16cm (6¼in) longer than the cushion back.

Estimating the fabric
Draw out the pattern pieces on graph paper following your measurements. Label the

pieces and mark the direction of the straight grain. Cut out.

On the same graph paper draw a long rectangle to the width of your chosen fabric. For plain fabric arrange the pattern pieces as closely as possible, keeping the straight grain of each 'fabric' piece parallel with the 'selvedges' of the graph paper.

For patterned fabrics mark in the length of the fabric repeat (see PATTERNED FABRIC) or where the main motifs fall, so that you can position each piece centrally over the pattern.

To find the amount of fabric needed, measure the length of the plan and convert it to full scale. Use the areas of fabric between the pattern pieces for piping or add extra fabric.

FRILLS AND PLEATS   205

PATTERNED FABRIC   217

LOOSE COVERS

Loose covers are not hard to make – the main pieces are cut out as large rectangles and pin fitted to the sofa, then trimmed down to the correct shape and size. A tuck-in allowance is added around the seat, which is pushed down around the seat to anchor the covers in place.

As all the pieces will look similar after cutting out, add a small sticky label to the wrong side to state what the piece is and the direction it should be placed on the sofa (this is essential for pile fabrics).

It may be necessary to join fabric widths together to obtain the width of the sofa back, front, seat and front panel. If this is the case, the seams should correspond with the edges of the seat cushions. With some plain fabrics, the material can be used sideways so this problem will not arise. Match patterns across seams and centralize any large motifs.

Make sure you choose a strong upholstery fabric that is tough and firmly woven.

BELOW A tailored loose cover gives a crisp neat look without being too formal and hides worn fixed upholstery underneath.

BOX-SHAPED LOOSE COVER

Cutting out the cover

Remove the seat and back cushions and calculate the dimensions of the sofa sections as explained in MEASURING UP. Cut out a rectangle of fabric for each piece, adding the correct pin-fitting/tuck-in allowance.

Mark the centre of the back, front, seat and front border of the sofa with a row of pins.

Start pinning the outside back in position on the sofa, matching the centre of the fabric piece with the marked centre of the sofa (**1**). Smooth the fabric over the back and pin to the side edges. Mark in the seamlines.

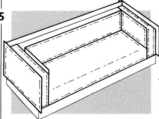

Pin the front to the sofa, with the tuck-in allowance at the base, and mark in the seamlines as before.

Pin the back box strip in place, matching centres and pinning to the front and the outside back pieces (**2**).

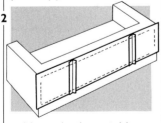

Next pin the outside arms and then the inside arms in place; remember

to position the tuck-in allowance at the base of the inside arms (**3**).

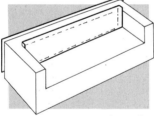

Place the arm box strip in position and pin to both the two arm pieces. Then pin the arm box strip to the back box strip and the outside arms to the outside back down the back corner seams (**4**).

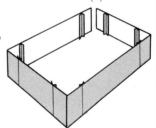

Pin the seat in place, matching the centres and with the tuck-in allowance at the back and sides. Pin the tuck-in allowances together round the seat.

Finally pin the front panel to the front of the seat and the arm box panels at each side (**5**).

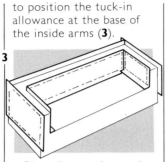

Remove the cover from the sofa. Tack and stitch it together in the same order as the pinning, leaving one outside back seam free for the opening. If you want the sofa to be piped, make up sufficient

covered piping and insert it between the fabric pieces before stitching (see PIPING).

Trim down the seam allowances to 1.5cm ($\frac{5}{8}$in) and zigzag stitch the raw edges together. Turn the cover to the right side and replace on the sofa and check carefully for fit. Mark round the base 14cm (5$\frac{1}{2}$in) from the floor and then make up the skirt (see MEASURING UP) as follows.

With right sides together, pin and tack the skirt and insert pieces together, beginning and ending with a half-insert and placing the other three between each section of skirt (**6**).

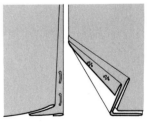

Fold the adjacent skirt piece over each half-insert so that the seamline lies 1.5cm ($\frac{5}{8}$in) from the insert edge. Then fold the sections towards each other, so that the seams meet together over each of the complete inserts (**7**). Pin, and tack along the top edge of the skirt.

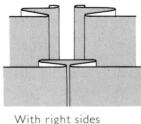

With right sides together, raw edges even and the half-inserts placed

either side of the back opening, place the skirt to the cover along the marked line. Pin, tack and stitch together, positioning an insert opening at each corner. Trim the excess fabric and zigzag the raw edges together to neaten.

Cut a self-fabric facing for the back opening 8cm (3in) wide and twice the length of the back opening.

At the top of the opening snip to the stitching line. With raw edges even, pin, tack and stitch the right side of the facing to the wrong side of the opening. Fold the facing over to the right side of the opening, turn under 1.5cm ($\frac{5}{8}$in) along the raw edge and then pin, tack and stitch the facing in place over the previous line of stitches. Fold the facing back to the wrong side of the opening. Stitch hooks and bars to either side (**8**).

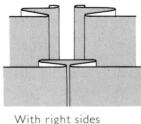

Zigzag stitch the raw base edge of the skirt and turn under a single 2.5cm (1in) hem. Pin, tack and stitch in place.

Making the cushion covers

Measure for the cushions (see MEASURING UP). For each cushion cut out a top and base piece, front, back and side gusset strip to

MEASURING UP	128

PIPING	203

FASTENING	208
NEATENING RAW EDGES	200
MEASURING UP	128

130

BELOW *This traditional sofa has been covered in a floral pattern but it would* look equally good encased in a bold, plain fabric.

equal the required size.

Cut the back gusset strip in half lengthways. Make up enough covered piping to fit around the cushion twice, allowing for joins (see PIPING).

Whipstitch the tape ends of the zip together at the top and bottom so they lie flat and will not part. Turn 1.5cm ($\frac{5}{8}$in) to the wrong side on the centre edges of the back gusset strip and press.

Place the folded edges of the back gusset strip close to the zip teeth. Pin, tack and stitch the strip to the zip, finishing at the end of each side of the zip.

With right sides facing, pin the gusset strips together, with the side strips in between the front and back strips. Tack and stitch, leaving 1.5cm ($\frac{5}{8}$in) open at each end of the front seams.

Beginning at the centre of the back edges, apply the piping to the cushion top and base, joining the loose ends (see PIPING) (**9**).

Pin, tack and stitch the gusset to the top of the cushion cover, matching the front seams against the unstitched corners. Open the zip. Stitch the other edge of the gusset to the base in the same way. Turn the cushion cover right side out. Place the cushion inside the cover.

TRADITIONAL LOOSE COVER

Make a rough sketch of the sofa and calculate the dimensions of each section of the cover (see MEASURING UP). However, omit the box strips and cut out a front arm piece instead. (The back and front of the sofa cover are stitched together.) The inside arm pieces can go round to a seam along the outside arm or to one underneath the scroll. The outside arm then begins at either of these points.

Pin each fabric piece on to the sofa and to each other in the same order as for the box-shaped cover.

When you get to the arms, pin the inside and outside arm pieces together, then pin on the

arm front. It may be necessary to take out some of the fabric fullness around the arm and the top back corners of the sofa. In each case, take out

the extra fabric in small evenly spaced darts (**1**).

Complete the cover and make up the cushion covers as explained in the previous instructions.

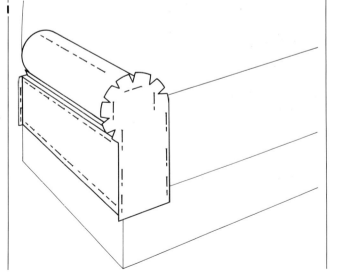

131

DECKCHAIR COVER

A simple white deckchair cover in heavy-weight cotton is enhanced with a touch of old lace. Use an old tray cloth that would otherwise lie unused and forgotten in a drawer. Cut in half, the lace-edged cloth provides decoration for the back and front edge of the chair when stitched in place. Otherwise make up two pieces of lace-trimmed fabric – in this way you can choose the type of lace you add to your chair.

BELOW *Re-covering a deckchair is a rewarding project because the results are so quick. Within a couple of hours you have a completely new chair.*

Making the cover
Remove the old cover from the chair and measure the length and width for the new one. Cut out one piece of fabric to the correct size, adding 4cm (1½in) to the width and 18cm (7in) to the length for casings.

Turn under a double 1cm (⅜in) hem down each long edge of the deckchair fabric. Pin, tack and stitch in place.

Turn under 9cm (3½in) along one short edge and then turn under a further 1cm (⅜in). Pin, tack and stitch along the hemline close to the hem edge to make the casing. Make another row of stitches across the casing 6mm (¼in) above the first row for added strength. If you are using an old tray cloth, cut it in half widthways and turn under the cut edges. Position one section near the top of the cover and the opposite half at the base, so that the lace edging will overhang the edges of the deckchair. Turn under any excess fabric at the sides of the tray cloth sections and pin, tack and stitch in place. If you do not have a suitable tray cloth, make up a piece of decorative work for each position. Cut two pieces of white fabric to fit the deckchair width, adding 4cm (1½in) to the width for hems. Turn under a double 1cm (⅜in) hem along the side edges; pin, tack and stitch. Topstitch strips of wide cotton lace across each piece. Turn the raw edge of each piece to the right side and pin and tack. Position a length of lace edging over each hem and topstitch in place. Position on the deckchair cover and stitch in place in the same way as the tray cloth pieces.

Knock out the dowelling rods from the deckchair frame. Slot them through the new cover and replace, glueing the rods back in position.

132

DIRECTOR'S CHAIR

Canvas chairs often look the worse for wear after a couple of seasons and while the frame might only need a good scrub, replacing the canvas may prove easier than cleaning. Measure the old canvas covering to obtain the dimensions of the new seat and back, but first check that it hasn't stretched. Fix the new seat in place with a heavy-duty staple gun. You will need to check that your sewing machine is equipped with a heavy-duty needle.

BELOW *Although generally used outdoors, the frames of these chairs can be polished or painted and covered with more sophisticated fabrics, such as pieces of kelim rug, for use indoors.*

Making the seat

Remove the old cover and measure across the seat both ways, not including hems/casings. Cut a piece of fabric to the required size, allowing 8cm (3in) for hems along the front and back edge and 4cm (1½in) for side turnings.

Neaten the front and back edges with zigzag stitching. Turn under the edges for 4cm (1½in) and stitch. Stitch each hem again to make a firm edge.

Close up the chair frame. Turn under 2cm (¾in) along each side of the seat fabric and staple it on to the frame (**1**). Open out the chair and check that the canvas is taut. If not, remove one side, turn under a wider hem and then re-staple in place.

Making the back

Measure across the stretched-out back both ways, not including hems/casings. Cut one piece to the required size, allowing 8cm (3in) for hems along the top and bottom edge and 24cm (9½in) for side casings. Neaten and turn under the top and bottom hems in the same way as above.

Turn under 12cm (4¾in) along each side edge; turn under the raw edge by 2cm (¾in). Stitch along the casing close to the raw edge foldline. Repeat 6mm (¼in) above the first row of stitching (**2**).

2

Slide the backrest battens into the casings and mark the positions of the screw holes on the canvas. Remove the battens. Either use a leather punch to make a hole at each mark or insert a large eyelet, which should strengthen the edges of the holes.

Slide the battens back into the casings and fasten in place.

1

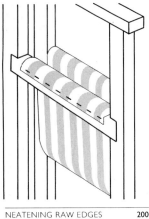

NEATENING RAW EDGES   200

DROP-IN CHAIR SEAT

Replacing a drop-in seat is not a daunting prospect. All you need is some webbing for the base, a layer of foam and then hessian and calico to complete the basic shape to which you add your choice of cover. Each layer is held in place with tacks. Make sure the webbing is taut as it is the foundation on which the seat rests. Cut out each piece of fabric on the straight grain and position any motifs centrally on the top cover. A layer of wadding can be added between the foam and the calico for a really smooth finish.

Webbing the frame

Remove the seat from the chair and strip the old upholstery. Measure across the seat and calculate how many strips of 5cm (2in) wide webbing will be needed to cover it; the gaps between the webbing should be no greater than the webbing width. Mark the position of each strip of webbing on top of the frame.

Working from the webbing roll, turn under 2.5cm (1in) and place over the first mark on the back of the frame 1.5cm ($\frac{5}{8}$in) in from the back edge. Fix in place with five tacks in the shape of a W (**1**). Pull the

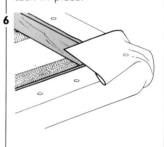

webbing over to the front rail and wrap around a small piece of wood, which will act as a stretcher. Pull the webbing over the frame until it is really taut, then hammer in three tacks in a row (**2**). Cut off

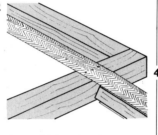

the webbing, leaving a turn-under of 2.5cm (1in). Fold under the loose end and hammer in place, making a W shape as before.

Repeat for each row of webbing. Weave the rows over and under the first set of strips when taking the webbing from side to side.

Attaching the padding

Cut a piece of hessian the size of the seat plus 1cm ($\frac{3}{8}$in) all round. Place the hessian centrally over the webbing (**3**). Turn up the edge, so the hessian lies just inside the frame

edges. Tack firmly in place, making neat folded corners.

Cut out a piece of 5cm (2in) thick foam 2.5cm (1in) larger than the seat. On the underside, cut away a triangle shape from along the edges. Cut out four 10cm (4in) wide strips of calico each length equal to a side of foam plus 15cm (6in).

Using a good fabric adhesive, stick half of each calico strip over the top edge of each side of the foam in turn, overlapping the strips at each corner (**4**). Leave to dry.

Next place the foam centrally on the seat and pull the calico strips round to the underside of the frame and temporarily tack in place at the centre of each side. Keep tightening the calico strips around the frame, adjusting the tacks until the foam looks smooth. Hammer in the tacks firmly. At the corners, fold the excess calico strips into tiny pleats and tack in place (**5**).

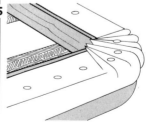

Cut out a piece of calico the size of the seat plus 10cm (4in) all round. Place it evenly over the foam and temporarily tack it in place at the centre of each side. Tighten the calico, smoothing down the seat to give a good rounded appearance. Hammer in the tacks. Pull the corners of the calico over each seat corner and tack, folding the two side pleats away from each corner (**6**). Cut away any excess calico from inside each pleat and tack in place.

Covering the seat and underside

Cut out the top fabric and cover the seat in the same way as the calico.

Cut a piece of hessian the same size as the underside of the seat. Turn under the raw edges and tack in place to the underside, making neat folded corners (**7**). Replace the seat in the chair. If it is difficult to fit, tap in place with a hammer, which should be well padded with cloth.

ABOVE *Drop-in chair seats
are not difficult to cover. A
gunmetal grey fabric
complements the bold
design of the chairs.*

135

TUFTED CUSHIONS

Simple cushions cover the sofa in a variety of colours, their centres tufted with chunky cotton thread. Use three layers of flock wadding for the filling. Tuft the wadding with a contrast colour thread, using a sharp, large-eyed tapestry needle.

TUFTED CUSHION IDEAS

Making the cushions

Cut out two pieces of fabric to the required size for each cushion, allowing 1.5cm (⅝in) on all sides.

Place the cushion pieces over each other with right sides together. Pin, tack and stitch all round, leaving a central opening in one side. Trim the seams and turn to the right side. Mark the centre of the cushion on both sides of the cover.

Cut out the layers of wadding to the correct size and place one on top of the other. Tack together loosely along the sides and diagonally across the middle before inserting into the cover. Turn in the opening edges in line with the remainder of the seam; pin, tack and slipstitch to close.

Thread the needle with three or four strands of heavy cotton and take a stitch through the cushion 1cm (⅜in) to the right of the marked centre, leaving loose ends of 5cm (2in). Bring the needle back through the cushion to the left of the marked centre. Take another stitch across the centre if necessary, to hold the wadding firmly in place. Cut off the threads level with the loose ends and tie a reef knot (see KNOTS) over the centre mark. Trim the thread ends to approximately 4cm (1½in).

STITCHES	197
KNOTS	209

ABOVE *Versatile and easy to make, these cushions can be piled high on a chair or used as floor seating.*

EIGHT CUSHION EDGINGS

Cord-edged cushion

For the front cut out one piece of fabric 41cm (16in) square. For the back cut out one piece 41cm by 8cm (16in by 3in) and one piece 41cm by 36cm (16in by 14¼in).

Place the back pieces with right sides together and raw edges even and pin and tack. Stitch in from both side edges for 5cm (2in). Press the seam open. Position a zip behind the tacked section (see FASTENINGS). Open the zip.

Place the cushion front against the back with right sides together. Pin,

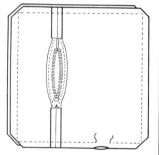

tack and stitch all round, leaving a small gap at the centre base. Trim and cut across the corners. Turn the cover to the right side.

Hand stitch the cord to the cover, crossing over and pushing the ends into the opening in the seam. At each corner twist the cord into a small loop.

Piped cushion with gathered corners

Follow the instructions for the corded cushion cover to cut out the fabric and make up the basic cover.

Before stitching, mark the seamline round the the cushion front. At each corner measure 5cm (2in) along each seamline and mark. Measure 2.5cm (1in) diagonally inwards from the corner point and mark. Join up the marks, gently rounding the shape.

Hand stitch along the marked corner line and pull up the thread to gather. Wrap the thread several times round the gathered corner and fasten off. Repeat, to gather up the remaining corners of the cushion.

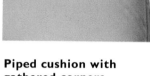
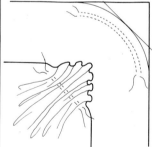

Measure round the front piece and make up a length of covered piping (see PIPING) in a constrast fabric equal to this measurement. Attach the piping.

Piped cushion with pleated frill

Follow the instructions for the corded cushion cover to cut out the basic cover pieces and make up the cushion back.

Measure round the front piece and make up a length of covered piping (see PIPING) in a contrast fabric equal to this measurement. Attach the piping.

From the main fabric cut out enough 14cm (5½in) wide fabric strips to fit twice round the cushion cover when joined together. Join the strips into a ring with plain flat seams. Fold the strip in half with wrong sides together. Divide the strip evenly into four sections. Make 10 equally sized knife pleats in each section (see PLEATS) with three narrower pleats at each corner. Pin and tack to the front cushion piece.

Open the zip and with right sides together, join the front to the back.

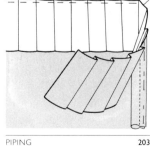

Cushion with ruched piping

Follow the instructions for the corded cushion cover to cut out the basic cover pieces and make up the cushion back.

For the ruched piping measure round the cushion front and cut out sufficient 3cm (1¼in) wide bias strips in self-fabric to equal twice this measurement when stitched together (see PIPING). Cut a length of piping cord to go round the cover, plus 5cm (2in). Fold the piping fabric evenly in half round the cord and secure at one end. Stitch alongside the covered cord for about 20cm (8in). Raise the machine foot, leaving the needle still in the fabric. Gently pull the piping cord through the fabric. Repeat until the complete length of piping cord has been ruched. Attach the piping to the cushion front.

Open the zip and, with right sides together, join the cushion back to the cushion front.

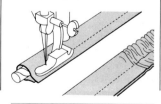

FASTENINGS   208   PIPING   203   PIPING   203   PLEATS   205   PIPING   203

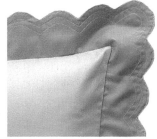

Cushion with bound frill

Follow the instructions for the corded cushion cover to cut out the basic cover pieces and make up the cushion back.

For the frill measure round the front cover 1.5cm ($\frac{5}{8}$in) from the outer edge and double this measurement. From the contrasting fabric cut one piece to this length by 8cm (3in). Join into a ring. Stitch pieces together if necessary to gain the length.

For the bound edge cut enough 3cm ($1\frac{1}{4}$in) wide bias strips (see PIPING) to equal the frill length when stitched together.

Position the made-up bias strip to one of the frill edges, taking a 1cm ($\frac{3}{8}$in) seam on the frill and a 6mm ($\frac{1}{4}$in) seam on the strip. Pin, tack and stitch in place. Press the strip over the frill edge and then turn under the remaining raw edge along the strip and slipstitch in place over the previous stitches. Gather and attach to the cushion front (see FRILLS).

Open the zip. Position the cushion back to the cushion front with right sides together. Stitch the pieces together, catching in the frill.

Cushion with single flange

Add 6.5cm ($2\frac{1}{2}$in) to the cover dimensions given in the instructions for the corded cushion cover. Cut out the cover pieces. Make up the back with a zip in the same way as for the corded cover, but stitch in from each side edge for an extra 6.5cm ($2\frac{1}{2}$in).

Open the zip. Place the cushion back to the cushion front with right sides together. Pin, tack and stitch the pieces together, taking a 1.5cm ($\frac{5}{8}$in) seam allowance. Trim and turn to right side through the zip.

Press the cover so that the seam falls on the edge. Pin and tack all round the cover 6.5cm ($2\frac{1}{2}$in) from the outer edge. Fit a twin needle on the sewing machine and, using matching thread, stitch all round the cushion cover along the tacked line.

Cushion with thick piping

Follow the instructions for the corded cushion cover to cut out the basic cover pieces and make up the cushion back.

Measure round the cushion cover 1.5cm ($\frac{5}{8}$in) from the outer edge and cut out and join sufficient 9cm ($3\frac{1}{2}$in) wide bias strips (see PIPING) to obtain this length. Cut out enough 8cm (3in) wide lengths of mediumweight wadding to equal the piping fabric length, allowing for joins. Join the wadding lengths (see WADDINGS).

Roll up the wadding tightly and place centrally on the wrong side of the piping fabric. Fold the

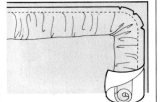

fabric evenly in half around the wadding; pin and tack close to the wadding. With raw edges even, attach the piping to the cushion front, snipping into the covering fabric at the corners.

Open the zip and, with right sides together, join the cushion back to the cushion front.

Cushion with scalloped edge

Follow the instructions for the corded cushion cover to cut out the basic cover pieces and make up the cushion back.

For the scalloped border cut out two 54cm ($21\frac{1}{4}$in) squares. Cut out the centres and discard, leaving an 8cm (3in) wide border.

Next make a paper pattern for the scalloped edge. Cut an 8cm (3in) wide strip of paper to the same length as one border side. Divide into 10 equally sized scallops, using the base of a glass. Cut out the pattern.

Place on the wrong side of each border piece and from the edge.

Place the border pieces with right sides together raw edges even. Pin, tack and stitch along the marked line. Trim any excess fabric and snip into the curves. Turn the border to the right side. Work three rows of evenly spaced topstitching 6mm ($\frac{1}{4}$in) apart.

Place the border to the right side of the cushion front, matching raw edges. Pin and tack. Open the zip and with right sides together, join the cushion back to the cushion front.

BALL AND SQUARE CUSHIONS

This neatly constructed ball cushion is made up in a similar way to a beach ball. You will probably have to make up a cushion pad as well, as it will be difficult to buy one this shape. A paper pattern makes the cutting out of the intricate design simpler than it looks.

Square cushions are straightfoward to make up – just sew right-angled corners and keep the stitching straight. If using a zip fastener, choose one that is about 5cm (2in) shorter than the cushion side.

Making the ball cushion
Begin by making a paper pattern of one segment of the cushion. On a piece of paper draw a line 44cm (17¼in) long and mark the centre. Draw an 11cm (4½in) line that crosses the centre, of equal length on both sides. Draw from the ends of the short line to the ends of the long line, marking an even rounded shape (**1**). Cut out the pattern.

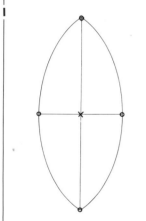

Using the pattern, cut out eight pieces of fabric, adding a 1cm (⅜in) seam allowance all round.

Pin, tack and stitch all the segments together to make a ball, leaving a central opening in one off-centre seam. Turn the ball right side out and fold along the central seam. Topstitch through two thicknesses of fabric close to the join to form a slight ridge that runs around the ball. (**2**).

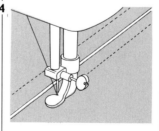

Make up a case for the cushion pad to the same size as the cushion, omitting the ridged seam and leaving an opening. Fit the case inside the cover and stuff it firmly. Turn in the opening edges and stitch to close.

Turn in the opening edges on the cushion cover in line with the remainder of the seam; slipstitch the folded edges together to close (**3**).

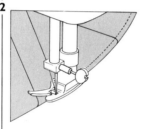

Making the square cushions
Decide on the cushion size. Cut two pieces of fabric for each cushion allowing 1.5cm (⅝in) for seams on all sides.

Place the cushion cover pieces with right sides together and pin and tack across one side. Stitch in from each side edge, leaving a central opening for the zip. Position the closed zip centrally behind the tacked section of the seam on the wrong side; pin, and tack (see FASTENINGS). Stitch the zip in place from the right side of the cover and then open the zip (**4**).

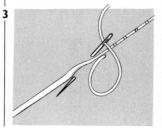

Pin, tack and stitch the remaining sides of the cushion cover. Trim and neaten the edges with zigzag stitching. Turn to the right side and insert the cushion pad. Close the zip and plump the cushion.

ABOVE *Not just cushions, but pieces of soft sculpture – and the ribbed fabric has a carved feel.*

QUILTED BOX CUSHION

The squishy inviting look of this box cushion is achieved by quilting the gusset strip and buttoning through the seat. Make the covered piping with a soft cord so the rows of quilting stitches pull it into a wavy shape. Lightweight wadding and muslin lining are needed for the gusset quilting. Cover the seat buttons with self-fabric.

Making the cushion

Measure the seat both ways and cut out two pieces of top fabric to this size plus 1.5cm ($\frac{5}{8}$in) seam allowances all round. Mark the button positions to correspond on both pieces of fabric.

For the gusset cut out four pieces of top fabric, each one the length of one side plus 3cm (1$\frac{1}{4}$in) by a width of 11cm (4$\frac{1}{2}$in).

Cut four pieces of wadding and four pieces of muslin the same size as the gusset pieces.

Place a piece of wadding then muslin behind one gusset piece (**1**); pin and tack. Quilt lines of stitching across the gusset piece at about 5cm (2in) intervals. Repeat, to quilt each gusset piece.

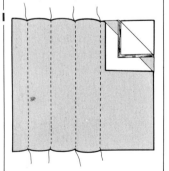

Pin, tack and stitch the gusset pieces together to make a ring, beginning and ending the stitching 1.5cm ($\frac{5}{8}$in) from each end of the seams.

Make up sufficient covered piping to fit around both top and bottom cushion cover pieces and stitch in place (see PIPING).

With right sides together and matching gusset seams to corners, pin, tack and stitch the gusset to the top cushion piece. Stitch the gusset to the base piece in the same way, leaving a central opening in one side.

Attach fastenings along the opening if desired. Place the cushion pad inside the cover. If no fastenings have been attached, turn in the opening edges in line with the remainder of the seam and slipstitch to close.

Cover the required number of buttons with fabric. Thread an upholstery needle with twine. At the first button position push the needle through the cover from the base to the top side, thread on a button and return to the base. Pull the needle clear of the fabric and thread on a button. Fasten with a slip knot (see KNOTS). Pull the twine until both knots sink into the cover and tie off around the shank. Trim off the ends of twine.

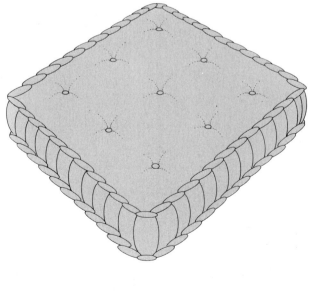

ABOVE *A plain wicker chair is made to look special with the addition of a piped quilted cushion in a nubbly cream fabric.*

143

ABOVE *These cushions are large enough to be used on the ground as loungers as well as providing very comfortable seating.*

WICKER SOFA CUSHIONS

Make a wicker sofa more comfortable with brightly coloured seating. If your sofa is very wide, pick a fabric that can be used sideways to avoid joining widths. Piping will give the cushions a longer life – use a self-fabric, or a contrasting one to highlight the edges. Stuff the cushions with shredded foam or a piece of foam or other filling encased in a made-up cushion pad cover. The finished cushion pad should be slightly larger than the outer cover to ensure a firm shape. As a precaution against suntan lotion or drinks spills, treat the fabric with a protector spray.

Making the cushions
For the cushion top and base measure across the seat from side to side and back to front. Cut out two pieces of fabric to equal this size plus 1.5cm (⅝in) seam allowance on all sides. For the front and side gusset strips allow the same length and width measurements as those of the top cover piece for the strip lengths and allow 13cm (5¼in) for each width. For the back gusset strip cut two pieces of fabric that measure the same length as the top cover piece by a width of 11cm (4½in).

Turn under a double 1.5cm (⅝in) hem along one long edge of each back gusset strip. Pin, tack and stitch. Place the back gusset strips one over the other with right sides together and pin, tack and stitch together alongside the hem for about 40cm

(16in) in from each side edge. Open out to single width.

Pin, tack and stitch all the gusset strips into a ring, beginning and ending the stitching 1.5cm (⅝in) from the ends of each seam.

Make up sufficient covered piping to fit round both the top and base cover pieces (see PIPING) and pin, tack and stitch in place, joining the loose ends of piping and snipping into the fabric at each corner.

Pin, tack and stitch the gusset to the top and base cover pieces. Trim and turn to the right side.

Blanket stitch press fastenings into the opening along the back gusset strip or stitch in touch and close spots. Make up a cushion pad to the same size and place in the cover.

Make up the cushion for the back in the same way.

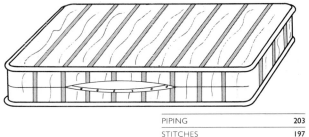

BUTTONED SQUAB CUSHIONS

Make the kitchen a cosier place with bright cushions – these ones are cut to fit the shape of the seat and filled with a 4cm (1½in) thick layer of foam to provide a comfortable seat on plain wooden chairs. To hold the cushions in place, make up self-fabric ties that fasten in bows around the chair back. Cover the buttons to match the chair fabric.

Making the squab cushions

First make a paper pattern of the chair seat. Using a piece of tracing paper that is slightly larger than the seat, trace around the seat edge. Remove the paper, fold it in half from back to front, and cut out the pattern; this ensures that the pattern will be an even shape. Replace the pattern on the seat and check for fit. Mark the position of the two outer struts.

Using the pattern, cut out two pieces of fabric for the seat top and base, allowing a 1.5cm (⅝in) seam allowance all round, and marking the strut positions on the fabric. Next mark the button positions on both pieces.

Make up sufficient covered piping to stitch round the top cover piece. Sew in position (**1**), joining the loose ends of piping on the back edge of the cover (see PIPING).

For the ties cut out two pieces of fabric each 60cm by 2cm (24in by ¾in). Fold

each piece in half lengthways with right sides together. Pin, tack and stitch down the length and across both ends, taking a 6mm (¼in) seam allowance and leaving a central opening. Trim the corners and turn to the right side. Turn in the central opening edges in line with the remainder of the seam and slipstitch to close.

Fold each tie in half and pin the folded edge in place at the marked positions on the base cover piece.

With right sides together and raw edges even, join the top and base pieces, leaving a central opening at the back (**2**). Trim the seams and turn the cover to the right side.

Place the pattern on a piece of 4cm (1½in) thick foam and mark the outline. Carefully cut out the foam using large dressmaker's shears. Place the foam inside the cover and turn in the opening edges in line with the

remainder of the seam; slipstitch to close.

Cover the buttons according to the maker's instructions.

Next thread an embroidery needle with a length of twine. Holding on to the loose twine end, push the needle through the cover from the base to the top side at the first button position. Thread on a button and return to the base. Pull the needle clear of the fabric and thread on another button. Tie the twine ends together with a slip knot (see KNOTS). Pull the twine until both buttons sink into the cover and tie off around the shank. Trim off the ends of twine and push them under the button. Repeat until all the buttons have been attached (**3**).

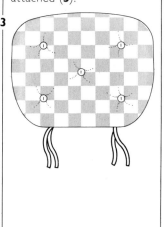

PIPING	203
STITCHES	197
KNOTS	209

ABOVE *The classic, tie-on, kitchen chair cushion looks its best made up in a fresh and easily washable fabric like gingham.*

FOUR SEAT CUSHIONS

Seat cushion with large bows

Place a sheet of tracing paper over the chair seat and mark round the edge. Remove the paper and fold in half from back to front. Keeping the paper folded, cut round the marked outline. Replace the pattern on the seat and check for fit. Mark in the positions of the struts.

Using the pattern, cut out two cushion pieces from the fabric, adding a 1.5cm ($\frac{5}{8}$in) seam allowance all round.

Measure round the front of the pattern from strut mark to strut mark and cut out an 8cm (3in) wide gusset strip to this length plus a 3cm ($1\frac{1}{4}$in) seam allowance. Measure the short distance between the marks and cut out the back gusset strip as before.

Make up enough covered piping to go round each cushion piece, allowing for joins (see PIPING).

For the bows cut out two pieces of fabric each 160cm by 18cm (63in by 7in). Fold each piece in half with the right sides together and cut the ends at a slant. Pin, tack and stitch all round, taking a 1cm ($\frac{3}{8}$in) seam allowance and leaving a central opening in one long side. Trim the seams and turn to the right side. Turn in the opening edges in line with the remainder of the seam and slipstitch.

Attach the piping to the edges of each cushion piece, joining the loose ends at the back (see PIPING). Pin, tack and stitch the gusset strips together into a ring. Pin, tack and stitch one edge of the gusset to one cushion piece, matching seams to strut marks. Repeat, to stitch the second cover piece to the opposite edge of the gusset, leaving an opening between the strut marks. Trim the seams and turn to the right side.

Pleat the centre of each bow strip to fit the gusset width. Place the strips centrally over the seams and stitch in place.

Place the pattern on a piece of 4cm ($1\frac{1}{2}$in) thick foam and mark round. Cut out the foam cushion and place it inside the cover. Turn in the opening edges in line with the remainder of the seam and slipstitch to close.

Seat cushion with touch and close straps

Follow the 'bow' cushion instructions to cut out and make up the basic cushion.

For the straps cut two pieces of fabric each 18cm by 6.5cm (7in by 2½in). Fold each strap in half with right sides together. Pin, tack and stitch all round, taking a 1cm (⅜in) seam allowance and leaving a central opening. Trim the seam and turn to right side. Fold in the opening edges in line with the remainder of the seam and slipstitch together.

Pin, tack and stitch a 3cm (1¼in) length of touch and close fastening to each strap end. Position the centre of the straps over the seams and stitch in place. Complete the cushion.

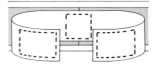

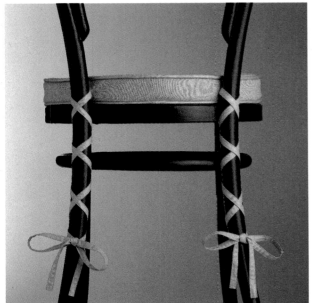

Seat cushion with ballerina ties

Follow the 'bow' cushion instructions to cut out and make up the basic cushion.

Cut out two pieces of fabric for the ties, each 160cm by 4cm (63in by 1½in). Fold the long raw edges of each tie to the centre and then fold in half. Tuck in the short edges. Pin, tack and topstitch all round.

Fold the ties in half and position each fold over a gusset seamline. Pin, tack and stitch in place. Complete the cushion.

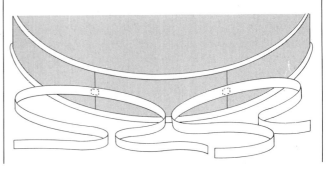

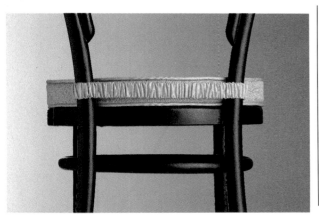

Seat cushion with elasticated strip

Follow the 'bow' cushion instructions to cut out and make up the basic cushion, attaching the strip before joining the gusset pieces.

For the elasticated strip measure from strut to strut around the outside and cut a piece of 2.5cm (1in) wide elastic to this length. Then cut an 8cm (3in) wide strip of fabric to the length of the elastic when extended. Fold the strip in half lengthways, right sides together. Stitch, taking a 1cm (⅜in) seam allowance. Turn to the right side, pressing the seam over the centre. Insert the elastic, stitching across each end to secure it.

With raw edges even, position each end of the elasticated strip centrally to the right side of each end of the front gusset. Complete the cushion.

TABLES

When covered with a cloth, any raised flat surface of adequate height can become a table – a supported board, a stool or even an old crate or beer keg. With a little imagination and the minimum of expense, the worn-out and even the thrown-out can be dressed up into a table fit for any occasion or place: it is the choice of fabric and the way it is draped that makes the transformation.

It takes only the simplest sewing stitches to make a basic covering – round, rectangular, square or oval. (It takes only scissors to cut a shape out of felt to make a simple cover-up.) But there are myriad ways to make the ordinary into something more special or spectacular. You can ornament the cloth with embroidery, cutwork or appliqué, or you can simply drape and arrange a cloth to give various folded sculptural effects. Nor is there any reason why a tablecloth should be just one fabric. You could try sewing together plain and printed fabric rectangles, or stitching a circular cloth from differently coloured or textured fabric segments. Use two layers of fabric – lace over a darker contrast. The hemlines can be worked with frills or scallops, edged with lace or fringes, or bound with satin ribbon. In fact once you start thinking of cloths as skirts, then almost anything that is done for a skirt will work for a tablecloth.

Floor-length cloths with stitched-on frills are a standard interior design feature, but the skirt of the cloth can just as easily be pleated. Simple kick pleats at the corners of a short tablecloth show off the good legs on a square table; a Victorian table with a central pedestal

is complemented by a formal skirt of flat tailored pleats.

Besides exploiting the way tablecloths are constructed, the fabric can be draped, knotted, swathed or layered. Give a round table a covering that skims the floor – several, if you like, with each successive layer shorter than the one underneath and complementary to it. If you have a square cloth that is large enough, knot it at the corners like a handkerchief. Catch up the sides of a round cloth at intervals to make flounces. On round tables with a central support the cloth can be gathered in round the support and tied with ribbons or pleated spirally and then secured. On four-legged tables the cloth can be wrapped around each leg and secured with a band or a bow, high or low down.

RIGHT *Anything can be used for a tablecloth, even a carpet. Protect it with a top cloth of gauze or organdy.*

RIGHT *A kitchen table needs a practical cloth that can be used at mealtimes and as a work surface. Traditional oilcloth fits the bill.*

Whatever your choice of decorative treatment, you must, of course, consider what the table is used for, whether the cloth must be easily washed, if it is to be a focal point or to blend into the surroundings. Occasional or side tables present the perfect opportunity to test out colours, textures and patterns because so little expense is involved.

Make the coverings match the curtains, the walls or the furniture, or let them stand out on their own as a splash or a beguiling island of colour in an otherwise plain room. Experiment with layers of different colours – shocking pink with deep red, green and turquoise, white with anything, black and white in an all-white room. Mix stripes and checks with florals. A black velvet undercloth topped with a small overcloth of white organdy offers an interesting and elegant textural combination. If the room is plain and a round table needs a cloth, then try a larger cloth in a butcher's stripe as the undercloth and add a topping of white linen. This little bit of drama may be just what is needed.

A scrubbed pine table set in a traditional or cosy kitchen immediately conjures images of relaxed mealtimes – with resultant wear and tear on the tablecloth. So opt for informal, easily washed fabrics like cotton damask or simple ginghams. Have a bit of fun and add crocheted cotton edgings to the cloth and napkins, and make cushions to match.

To make it more workmanlike, the corners of a square kitchen tablecloth can be mitred to fit the table and cut short to reveal and make accessible drawers underneath. Embroider a scalloped or zigzagged edge, or trim it with contrasting piping or cotton lace.

In rooms where you are more likely to entertain (and this includes the kitchen/dining area, combined living- and dining-rooms, and bedsits as well as dining-rooms) you can really go to town and treat the table as the focal point of the room. Place a smaller cloth on top of the main one and then make mats to contrast or co-ordinate with the cloth underneath. Think in terms of checks with stripes,

Pockets in a picnic cloth also stop it blowing away.

RIGHT *The deep blue of an indigo-dyed cloth is a suitable foil for the brightly coloured flowers in this city garden.*

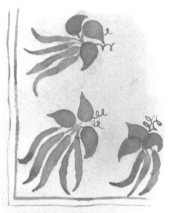

Create your own design using a familiar motif.

ABOVE *A white tablecloth
and matching napkins look
clean and fresh and make the
perfect background for food
and wine.*

patterns with plains, bright and varied colours on top of a plain cloth, white mats on black cloth as an extreme.

Circular cloths look good with a stencilled border: take food as your theme and stencil a stylized vegetable border, a frieze of runner beans hanging down in a row from garlands of leaves, tendrils and scarlet bean flowers.

If a highly polished dining-room table needs its surface protected with a tablecloth, think of making a quilted cloth and topping it with a series of interchangeable ones that can match the plates, the flowers, the chair covers or even the food when the theme is, say, a red and white dinner. Alternatively, cover the surface with a floor-length protective cloth, perhaps in bright felt, and then cover this with another cloth in white or a contrasting colour and catch up the sides of this top cloth to show the coloured felt beneath.

A table that is needed for food or drinks may have the top protected with a sheet of glass cut to size. You could think of taking advantage of this protection to display something quite fragile or precious beneath the glass – a fabric collage, a piece of embroidery or a shawl. You could also do the same for a dressing table.

Following another principle of the dressing table, you can store bottles and other items you may not want on permanent display on a shelf underneath a round curtained table topped with an overcloth. Fit a curtain track around the underside of the table and attach the mock undercloth as you would a curtain, making sure the opening edges overlap generously and the opening is positioned inconspicuously when the table is *in situ.*

The cloth itself can be used for storage and the table done away with altogether when going for a picnic. Spread out a sturdy cotton cloth on the ground to which have been attached canvas pockets that hold the cutlery, plates, glasses, salt and pepper and so on. The whole cloth can then be rolled up tightly at the end of the picnic and secured with tapes stitched to the edges.

MEASURING UP – TABLES

The overhang measurement on all tables should include the hem allowance.

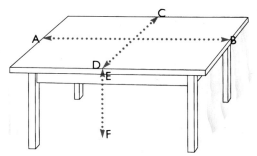

Rectangular tables
Measure the distance **A–B** and **C–D** from edge to edge, then add twice the overhang **(E–F)** to both these measurements.

Making large cloths
Panels usually have to be attached to either side of a centre width to obtain the correct size of cloth and to avoid a centre seam. Double the length needed to make the cloth if you are attaching side panels measuring up to one half width. Triple the length if the panels are between a half and a complete width. Include a 1.5cm ($\frac{5}{8}$in) seam allowance for every edge that has to be joined.Extra fabric should be allowed for matching patterns across seams.

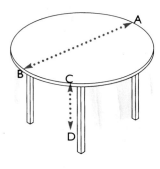

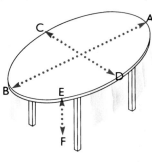

Round tables
Measure the diameter **A–B** across the centre of the top from edge to edge, and then add twice the overhang **C–D** to this measurement.

Oval tables
Measure the distance **A–B** and **C–D** from edge to edge at the widest point and then add twice the overhang **E–F** to both these measurements.

158

ROUND SEAMED CLOTH

A tablecloth is an excellent way of injecting a blaze of colour into a room or covering an undistinguished table. It gives a sense of occasion to any meal, even a simple al fresco picnic in the garden.

Panels have been attached to a centre width to obtain a deep overhang on this tablecloth. Buy extra fabric if matching patterns across seams. The napkins are plain squares of fabric with narrow hems.

Making the cloth

Cut two lengths of fabric to the required size (see MEASURING UP), allowing for a 1.5cm ($\frac{5}{8}$in) hem.

Fold one piece in half lengthways and cut along the fold to form two half widths. Join the widths to the centre panel with flat fell seams and press.

Fold the fabric in four and press, matching the outer edges and seams. Then wrap a length of string around a drawing pin and push it through the centre of the folded fabric (**1**).

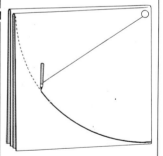

Tie the other end of the string to the pointed end of a pencil or fabric marker pen so that the length equals the radius of the tablecloth when the string is pulled taut and the pencil upright. Draw an arc.

Cut along this line

through all thicknesses and open out.

Stitch round the cloth 1.5cm ($\frac{5}{8}$in) from the edge. Press under the fabric along this stitched line, easing it as you press. The stitching should be just on the wrong side of the cloth. Turn under the raw edge 6mm ($\frac{1}{4}$in) and press. Tack in place and hem by hand or machine stitch close to the raw edge foldline (**2**).

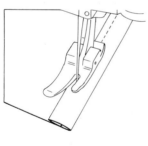

Making the napkins

Cut four 33cm (13in) squares of fabric and fold a double 6mm ($\frac{1}{4}$in) hem all round. Pin, tack and stitch close to the hemline (**3**).

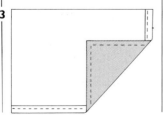

ABOVE *Choose fresh-looking country cottons like this Provençal print for use outdoors.*

MEASURING UP   158

SEAMS   200

CO-ORDINATED TABLECLOTHS

The lavishly draped undercloth is oval in shape. If your table is wide, buy 140cm (54in) wide fabric to avoid joining more than two extra panels to either side of the centre width to obtain the floor folds. The overcloth consists of a main panel of background fabric that has been appliquéd with two rectangles of contrast fabric and a corner block. The outer contrast rectangle is made from a double thickness of fabric and has been stitched to the edges of the cloth to form a top border. Position any seams in the overcloth under the appliqué strips.

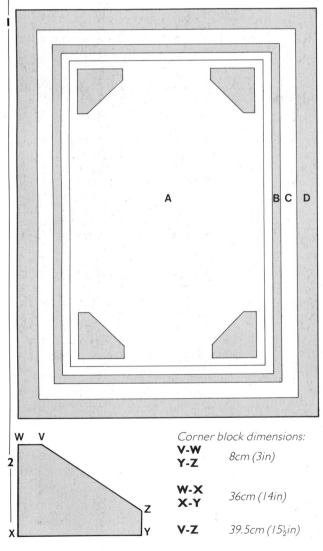

Corner block dimensions:

V-W **Y-Z**	8cm (3in)
W-X **X-Y**	36cm (14in)
V-Z	39.5cm (15½in)

Cutting out the cloths

Calculate the amount of fabric required for the two cloths (see MEASURING UP). For the overcloth, the overhang should measure 32cm (12½in) and for the undercloth, the distance from the table top to the floor, plus a floor drape section of at least 50cm (20in). Cut the fabric lengths for the two cloths and join any side panels with flat fell seams.

Shaping the undercloth

Fold the undercloth in four, matching seams and outer edges and press.

Cut a paper pattern to fit one quarter of the table top exactly. Lay it on the fabric, matching the right angle with the folded corner. Pin firmly in place.

Measure the depth of the overhang from the pattern edge, marking a parallel curve along the fabric in pins or tailor's chalk. Cut along the curve through all thicknesses (**3**).

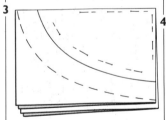

Open out and hem as for the ROUND SEAMED CLOTH, taking a 2.5cm (1in) hem allowance. Remove the tacking stitches and iron the quarter creases smooth to finish.

Cutting out the appliqué shapes and border

The strips can be cut widthways and joined to save fabric. Take a 1cm (⅜in) seam allowance when applying or joining appliqué and border pieces.

Cut two 22cm (8¾in) wide border strips in **D** that measure the width of the cloth plus 22cm (8¾in). Cut another two strips that measure the length plus 22cm (8¾in).

In **C** cut two appliqué strips 10cm (4in) wide by the length and width; in **B** cut two strips 6cm (2¼in) by the length and width less 22cm (8¾in).

Next cut a paper pattern to fit the dimensions of the corner block (**2**) and cut out four shapes.

Making the overcloth

First join the **C** and **B** strips at the corners to form two rectangles.

At each end of each strip fold up the short raw edge to the opposite long raw edge and press (**4**). Unfold and cut along the creased line.

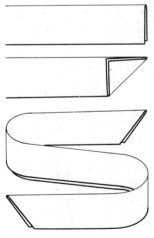

Take each set of strips and place the angled ends together, raw edges even, right sides facing. Stitch

across the ends, leaving
1cm (⅜in) unstitched at the
inner corner.

Press under the inner
edge of the **C** rectangle
and lay it on top of the
cloth with the right sides
facing upwards and raw
edges even. Pin and tack in
position and then topstitch
along the inner edge.

Turn under the inner
and outer edge of the **B**
rectangle and position it
3cm (1⅛in) from **C**. Tack in
place and then topstitch
the rectangle to the main
fabric along both edges.

Fold the **D** strips in half
lengthways with the right
sides out and raw edges
even; press. Mitre the
corners in the same way as
above, folding up the short
raw edge to the long
folded edge. Unfold the
strips and place the
pointed ends together,
raw edges even, right sides
together. Pin, tack and
stitch together around the
pointed ends (**5**), leaving
1cm (⅜in) unstitched at
either end of each seam.

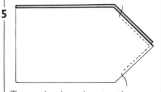

5

Turn the border to the
right side, pushing out the
mitred corners. Press
under the inner raw edge
on the upper and lower
sides and pin, tack and
topstitch the border to
the main tablecloth.

Next press under the
edges of the corner blocks
and position at each
corner with the sides
6.5cm (2½in) from
rectangle **B**. Pin, tack and
topstitch.

ABOVE *For entertaining on
a grand scale, the table is
decked with sumptuous folds
of fabric decorated with
stylish yet simple appliqué.*

161

CUTWORK TABLECLOTH

Ideal fabrics for this delicate embroidered cloth are close weaves like lawn, cambric or fine linen. Use a frame for ease of working and sharp embroidery scissors for the cutwork motifs. Part of the cutwork design is filled in with voile appliqué; only small scraps of fabric are needed. Embroidery silk should be used on the satin-stitched portion of the design if it is worked by hand.

RIGHT *The motif in the cloth echoes the wall stencil. Take inspiration from your surroundings and create a motif of your own.*

Making the cloth
Cut out or make up a rectangular cloth following the instructions given in MEASURING UP, joining any side panels with flat fell seams. The dimensions must be calculated so that the scallops can be repeated in full all round the cloth, with a three-sided scallop centred over each corner.

Positioning the motif
Fold an A4 sheet of tracing paper in quarters. Unfold and trace the half motif, matching the intersecting crease lines against the registration mark. Turn the tracing paper over, line up the crease lines with the registration mark, and trace the other half of the motif (**I**).

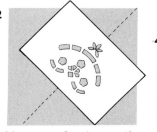

Mark the motif placings on the cloth with pins or masking tape (see STENCILLING A STRAIGHT BORDER). Use the sides and corners of the tracing paper in the same way as those of the stencil block.

The motif should be centred across the corners of the cloth (see POSITIONING A STENCIL ACROSS A CORNER). Align the vertical crease in the tracing paper with the midpoint when positioning the motif over the diagonal (**2**).

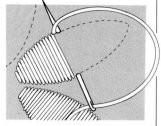

Next transfer the motif on to the cloth (see PRICKING AND POUNCING).

Applying the appliqué
Place a small square of fine voile over an appliqué motif and trace directly on to the fabric. Cut out the voile shape.

Stretch the ground fabric over an embroidery frame and tack the motif in position. Work round the edges in buttonhole

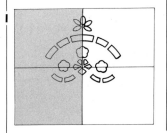

stitch (**3**), then carefully trim away the main fabric from the underside. Repeat until the appliqué sections are completed.

Making the eyelets
Stitch around the outside edges of the cutwork eyelets with small running stitches. Snip through the centre (**4**).

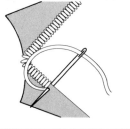

Turn the excess fabric to the back (**5**), overcast (see EMBROIDERY) around the edge, and then trim (**6**).

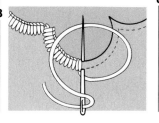

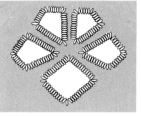

Embroidering the petals and scallops
Fill in each petal of the embroidery by hand, stitching away from the centre in close, even satin stitch (**7**) (see EMBROIDERY).

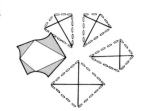

Next make a card template of the scallop section. Repeat the pattern on a large piece until you have a suitable length to work with.

Draw around the template with a pencil along the edge of the cloth. Stitch just inside the outline to make a firm edge. Then work close machine zigzag around the scallops to look like satin stitch (**8**). Alternatively, embroider by hand. Trim the excess fabric down to the embroidered edge.

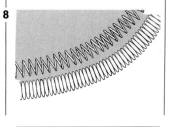

These scallop shapes are full size. Alternate them along the edge of the tablecloth.

A *embroidery*
B *cutwork*
C *appliqué*

SIX NAPKIN EDGINGS

Napkin with zigzagged edge

For each napkin cut one piece of fabric 41cm (16in) square. Next make a paper pattern to correspond to one side of the napkin. Cut out a piece of paper 41cm by 4cm (16in by 1½in). Divide the length up into eight equally sized sections, with the corner point being half the size of a side section. Mark a 2.5cm (1in) deep triangle in each section. Cut out the pattern.

Position the pattern along one edge of the napkin with points against the fabric edge and mark round. Repeat along each edge. Stitch all round the napkin just inside the marked line. Trim off the excess fabric from around the design following the marked lines. Make close zigzag stitches all round the edges to form satin stitch, or embroider by hand (see EMBROIDERY).

Bordered napkin

For each napkin cut out a piece of fabric 41cm (16in) square. For the border cut out a 41cm (16in) square in contrasting fabric. Cut out the centre of this square and discard, leaving a 3cm (1¼in) wide band.

Place the contrast band with its right side to the wrong side of the napkin. Pin, tack and stitch the pieces together around the outer edge, taking a 1cm (⅜in) seam allowance. Trim and turn the complete band to the right side of the napkin.

Turn under the inner edge by 1cm (⅜in), snipping into the allowance at the corners.

Pin, tack and topstitch along the inner edge. Topstitch along the outer edge of the napkin to match. Add three more evenly spaced rows of topstitching round the napkin in between the first two rows. Fasten off the threads securely.

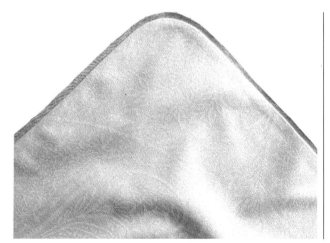

Napkin with bound edge

For each napkin cut a piece of fabric 41cm (16in) square. Place a small plate against the first corner with the edges matching both edges of the napkin, and mark round the corner. Cut out. Fold the napkin in half and mark the next corner and cut out. Repeat, to mark and cut round each corner in turn.

Measure round the edge of the napkin. Cut out and make up a 2cm (¾in) wide bias strip in contrasting fabric to this length (see PIPING), adding 1cm (⅜in) for the join. With right sides together and raw edges even, position the binding around the edge of the napkin, overlapping the loose ends of the binding and turning under one end to neaten. Attach the binding strip to the napkin, taking a 6mm (¼in) seam allowance (see APPLYING BINDING).

Appliquéd napkin

For each napkin cut a piece of fabric 41cm (16in) square. Turn under a double 6mm ($\frac{1}{4}$in) hem all round the napkin; pin, tack and stitch.

Trace the appliqué motif and transfer it on to the contrast fabric. Lightly outline the motif on the corner of the napkin. Cut out a piece of bonding webbing slightly larger than the outline of the motif and iron on to the back of the contrast fabric. Cut out the individual appliqué shapes and bond them to the napkin.

Stitch round each shape close to the edge. Using three strands of matching embroidery cotton, work buttonhole stitch around each shape in turn then work single lazy daisy stitches (see EMBROIDERY) round the shapes.

Scallop-edged napkin

For each napkin cut out a piece of fabric 41cm (16in) square.

Make a paper pattern of the scalloped edge. Cut a piece of paper 41cm by 4cm (16in by 1$\frac{1}{2}$in). Divide the paper up into 10 equal sections. Choose a small drinking glass that fits the section width and, with the glass edge just touching the paper edge, mark round the base to make a scallop shape in the first section. Repeat in each width so that the scallops join together. Cut out the pattern.

Place on each side of the napkin in turn and mark the scalloped edge on the wrong side. At each corner two shapes will combine to form a rounded corner.

Set the sewing machine on an open zigzag stitch and work round the napkin along the marked line.

After stitching, trim away the excess fabric. Using three strands of matching embroidery cotton, work buttonhole stitch round the edge.

Napkin with bullion knotted edge

Cut out one piece of fabric 39cm (15$\frac{1}{2}$in) square for the centre section. Turn under a double 1cm ($\frac{3}{8}$in) hem, folding the corners into mitres. Pin, tack and stitch.

For the outer edge, cut a 46cm (18in) square of fabric. Cut out and discard the centre, leaving a 5cm (2in) wide border. Fold the border in half with right sides together and pinch up the corners to form evenly sized darts. Stitch the darts, then trim them and turn the border to the right side. Turn in both the inner edges of the border for 6mm ($\frac{1}{4}$in); pin, tack and stitch together. Position the border around the napkin. Using three strands of matching embroidery cotton and beginning at one corner, work bullion bars (see EMBROIDERY) around the napkin, joining the border to the inner section.

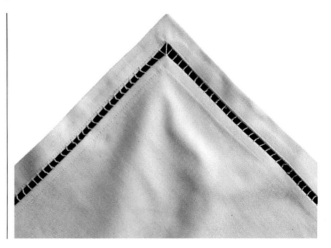

BEDS

How you dress your bed will depend on the atmosphere you want to create and the type of bed you own. Dressing a bed is easy – like curtains, it is just a matter of hemming and seaming together widths of fabric. Minimal beds such as futons and stark modern designs in wood or tubular metal look best covered with a simple duvet and matching pillowcase, which can compensate for their plainness by being made in strong contrasting colours or boldly printed fabric. Some beds by their very structure – a four-poster for example – demand a grandiose treatment that measures up to their flamboyant style. Even the simplest divan can easily be transformed with a canopy, the right coverings and masses of frilled pillows, into the type of bed that might have starred in *Gone with the Wind* – though when a bedroom doubles as study or sitting-room, you might want a less arresting bed that makes a comfortable seat.

The neat lines of a divan suit a tailored, functional room. The bed can be transformed into a sofa during the day by covering both the base and the top in the same close-fitting fabric. If the base is already covered in an acceptable fabric, such as mattress ticking, this provides a cue to copy for the bedcover, slip covers for the pillows and perhaps a bolster, too. To make this less severe, add piping of a contrasting colour and hang a tassel at either end of the bolster. Alternatively, cover the spring base with a close-fitting valance or give it a little detailing with flat pleating, and finish the bed with a cover to match. These simple straightforward ideas can be made more elaborate by adven-

RIGHT *Traditional bedclothes such as white sheets, bulging eiderdowns and crochet bedspreads look good with an iron bedstead.*

RIGHT *A duvet can look like an heirloom. Embroider it, trim it with lace or make the top side of the cover from patchwork.*

BELOW *A double-ended Empire bed can be given a frothy, lacy treatment or dressed in more tailored lines with a crisp striped fabric.*

turous choice of colour and pattern. For example, the cover can be in a fabric that sharply contrasts with the valance: one plain and the other patterned, or striped and checked, black and white. Valances can be banded or bordered, given kick pleats of a contrast colour or frilled. Imagine a box-pleated valance – each pleat should be quite wide – and a brilliant pinky red duvet with tape ties.

A distinctive colour theme is useful when wanting to escape the boudoir image. School uniforms, liveries, even racing colours often

suggest bold or subtle variations. The tailored bed can be dressed in a uniform that matches the chairs and curtains. Use a main colour throughout, backed up with a secondary one. For example, a navy duvet would look good piped with white, with a navy valance. Do the same with the chairs, but vary the theme by making the curtains white edged with blue. Add a blue roller blind if you need to sleep in the dark. All very tailored and shipshape.

A simple backdrop curtain hung behind the bed can help to make a focal point at the head of the bed besides acting as an unobtrusive headrest. Make this to match the bedspread or curtains. Slip covers for bed heads using the same stuff as the bedcover or valance will make the bed and head into a unified whole. They can be simply closed with a zip or given a flourish with tied closures.

Although the practical reasons for having curtains and canopies are now redundant, hanging and arranging drapes over a bed are a very effective way of turning an ordinary bed into a focal point. A bed can be placed alongside a wall and a canopy suspended from a central ridge pole, tent fashion, so that drapes hang at either end of the bed in a simplified Empire look. The wall itself can be lined or hung with contrasting or coordinating material: brown velvet with golden satin; a lacy white bed in a lacy white enclosure with a Persian blue wall; a gingham checked bed with a flocked voile drape.

Half testers can be created by suspending a framework from the ceiling and draping the frame with, perhaps, swathes of muslin looped up with clusters of flowers for a romantic effect. The tester can also have fabric stretched over it and can be completed with a scalloped edge or fringing. Curtain rails can be bent into a corona shape above which a small dome can be built up, or around which curtains can be pulled. A curtain pole can also jut centrally out from the wall over the bed, with a length of fabric or shawl thrown over it to hang gracefully at either side.

LEFT *Bedcoverings can be made to fit in with the decorative theme of a room. Here the cover matches the curtains and the bold splashy print looks right against the knobbly bamboo bed.*

171

Four-posters are constructed from kits or with curtain rods. As very heavy hangings are not nowadays needed for warmth, play up a stark silhouette with filmy drapes. Let curtains drop down from the rods vertically instead of drawing them along the rails, and tie them up in loose bundles by means of tapes during the day. Pull lengths of sheer fabric across the frame to form a tester, and knot the ends to each post. Make sure any of these arrangements looks equally good when you are lying in bed.

Bunk beds are mostly used for children but it is a pity to restrict their use to the younger generation, as they are good space savers and make excellent spare beds. Put them into alcoves to enclose them, hang them around with curtains, pad the recessed walls with quilting or frame them with stencilling copied from the bed coverings. Treat the space of each bunk bed as a miniature room, and put in shelves lined in the same fabric as the walls and bedcovers and add individual lamps to each enclosure, the type that can be mounted on the wall.

Don't confine your inventiveness to the external dressing of the bed: extend the co-ordination of colour, pattern and trimming detail to the bedclothes themselves. Printed dress fabric can be used to make sheets, if you can get some that can stand up to constant washing and you don't mind it being patterned only on one side. Imagine red and white sprigged cotton folded over a red fluffy blanket. Plain sheets lend themselves to embroidery along the edge, especially crocheted lace. Think in terms of trimmings, piping, grosgrain ribbon, inset flowery borders, loops and ties for pillowcases. Anything that can be done to trim a sheet or pillowcase can also be done to a duvet cover. But don't forget that the first criterion for a bedroom is that it should induce sleep. Think twice about choosing patterns that excite rather than relax, or you may find yourself saying, like Oscar Wilde, that either you or the pattern must go.

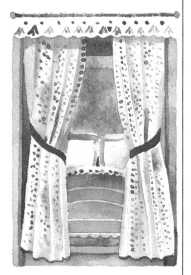

Nowadays lightweight drapes can be used on four-posters.

RIGHT *Patchwork provides the decorative theme in this child's bedroom. The walls and bed are covered with traditional patchworks and the curtains have been made up to blend in.*

MEASURING UP – BEDS

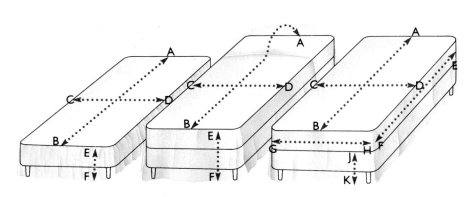

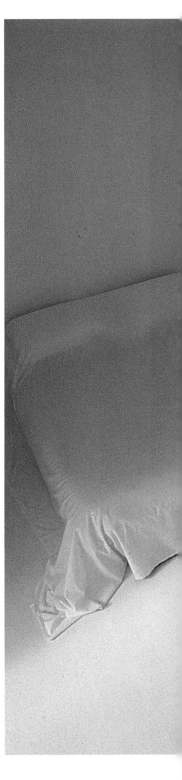

Valance

Remove all the bedclothes and mattress. Measure the length **A–B** and the width **C–D** of the bed base. Add a 1.5cm ($\frac{5}{8}$in) seam allowance to the side and bottom edges and a 2cm ($\frac{3}{4}$in) hem allowance to the top edge. For the depth of the skirt **E–F** measure from the top of the bed base and add a hem and seam allowance. The skirt width **G–H** will vary according to whether it is frilled or pleated and it is attached to the centre panel on three sides.

Lined throwover bedspread

Always measure for a bedspread with the usual bedclothes and pillows in position. Measure the length **A–B** and width **C–D** and then add the depth **E–F** to the length and twice this measurement to the width, plus a seam allowance of 1.5cm ($\frac{5}{8}$in) to all sides. The depth measurement will depend on how much overhang is required.

Add extra fabric to the length if the bedspread is to be tucked under the pillow(s) at the front.

Join side strips to a main panel to obtain a wide bedspread, if possible positioning the seams at the edges of the bed. Add on a seam allowance to each edge when cutting out the fabric pieces.

Extra fabric must be allowed if matching patterns across seams.

Fitted divan cover

Measure for the cover over the bedding.

Measure the bed top length **A–B** and width **C–D** and add a 1.5cm ($\frac{5}{8}$in) seam allowance to each side. Measure the long and short sides of the mattress lengthways **E–F** and widthways **G–H**. Cut two long and two short strips for the welt, adding a 1.5cm ($\frac{5}{8}$in) seam allowance to all sides. Measure the desired depth of the skirt **J–K** from the bottom of the mattress and make up a suitable strip of fabric if attaching pleats or frills (see FRILLS AND PLEATS). For a skirt that is split at the corners, cut two long and two short sections to the length of the welt strips, the width equal to the desired depth of the skirt. Allow for a 1.5cm ($\frac{5}{8}$in) seam on the top edge and a hem or seam allowance on the other three according to whether the skirt is to be lined or not.

FRILLS AND PLEATS   205

LINED THROWOVER BEDSPREAD

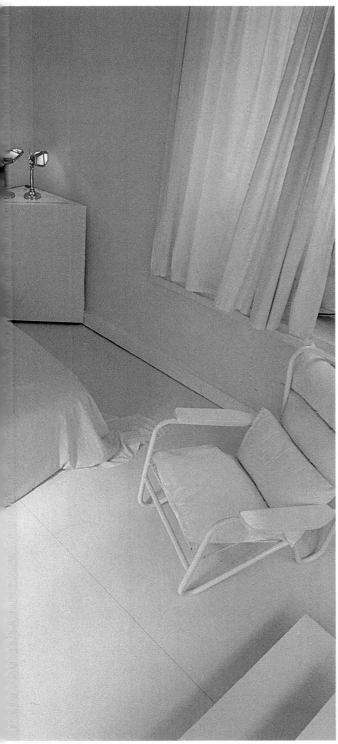

Simplest of all bed linen to make, a throwover bedspread is made from a rectangle of fabric that drapes the bed loosely down to the floor. Almost any type of fabric can be used for a plain lined cover, provided it is crease-resistant and has enough body to hang well.

Making the bedspread

Measure the bed as shown in MEASURING UP. From the top and lining fabrics cut a centre panel and two side strips to the correct length and width.

With right sides together and raw edges even, join the side strips of top fabric to the centre panel top fabric. Repeat with the pieces of lining fabric. Matching the raw edges and seams and with right sides together, pin and tack the top and lining sections together, leaving a 56cm (22in) central opening at the bottom end (**I**). Stitch and clip the corners.

Turn the bedspread right side out, press the outer edge, and turn in the opening edges in line with the remainder of the seam. Slipstitch to close.

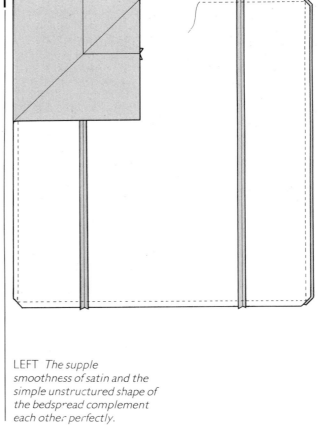

LEFT *The supple smoothness of satin and the simple unstructured shape of the bedspread complement each other perfectly.*

MEASURING UP   174

QUILTED BEDCOVER

Lightweight fabrics are best for this machine-quilted cover which is worked in four manageable sections and joined before lining. The middle layer of the cover is made from heavyweight wadding stitched to a backing of cheap lining fabric. The underside of the cover is lined with cotton sheeting or you can line it to match the top fabric.

Making the bedcover

Measure the bed in the same way as for a throwover bedspread (see MEASURING UP).

Divide the width measurement by four and add 8cm (3in) to this measurement to obtain the width dimension of each of the strips that make up the bedcover. Cut four each of these strips from the wadding and backing fabric to measure the length of the cover plus a 4cm (1½in) seam allowance on either end. A generous seam allowance is necessary as the quilting stitches draw the fabrics into the wadding. Next cut a piece of lining fabric that measures the complete width of the bedcover by the length plus a 4cm (1½in) seam allowance on all sides.

Mark the seamlines in tailors' chalk on the right side of the top fabric and then rule evenly spaced lines within the seamlines to form a grid.

Sandwich the wadding between the backing and top fabric and tack together at the raw edges and across the centre (**1**).

Test the stitch size and thread on a scrap piece of quilting first. Then machine stitch along the lines of each strip through all layers, starting and finishing at the tacked seamlines. Next remove the tacking and trim away any wadding from the seam allowances.

With all raw edges even and right sides together, pin, tack and stitch the strips together along their length. Open out and press. Keeping the distance between the lines of quilting even, topstitch along one side of each seam.

Join the lining fabric if it has been cut in separate widths. Attach to the quilted section as shown in LINED THROWOVER BEDSPREAD.

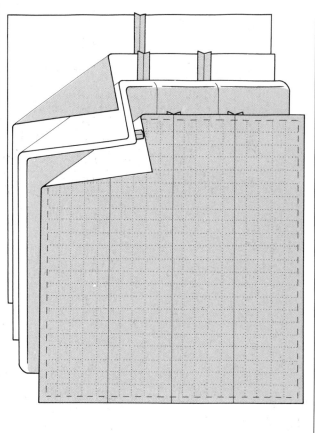

QUILTED BEDCOVER

ABOVE *A lightweight covering in summer and cosy extra warmth in winter, this quilt gives a sumptuous look to the starkest room.*

177

FRILLED VALANCE

The soft nostalgic look of a frilled valance complements a beautiful old bedstead and provides a decorative cover for the base and legs of an ordinary divan.

The skirts of the valance can also be box pleated or left straight with a deep inverted pleat at each corner. Choose the weight of fabric that is most appropriate for the style. Lightweight washable fabrics are best for an unlined gathered skirt, and cheap lining fabric can be used for the section concealed under the mattress. As the fabric in the photograph is not widely available, a frill of checked tea-cloths is suggested as a fun and ready-hemmed alternative.

Making the valance
Calculate the number of cloths needed to make a valance that covers the bed on three sides. Allowing for 1cm (⅜in) seams at each join, the joined-up cloths should measure four times the length of the bed and twice the width. They are stitched together along the short edges. A standard tea-cloth measures approximately 74cm × 51cm (29in × 20in), but check the dimensions before you buy any.

Measure and cut out the centre panel as instructed in MEASURING UP. Cut the bottom corners into a curve, using a saucer (see PIPED DAY BED COVER). Turn under a double 1cm (⅜in) seam along the top edge.

Measure from the top edge of the bed base to the floor and trim off any unwanted fabric from one long edge of each tea-cloth less a 1.5cm (⅝in) seam allowance. Join the short edges of the cloths.

Fold the strip in six and

mark each fold with a pin. Work two rows of gathering stitches along

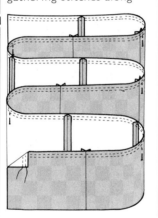

the raw edge, stopping and restarting the stitching at the dividing points (**1**).

Measure the distance along three sides of the centre panel (**G–H** in diagram **3** of MEASURING UP). Divide this distance into six equal sections and mark on the edge of the fabric with a pin.

With right sides together and raw edges even, attach the centre panel to the side strip at the pin marks and gather the fabric evenly between (**2**). Pin, tack and stitch.

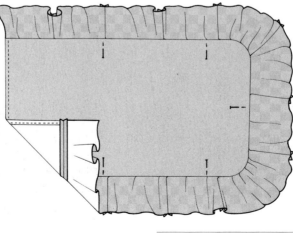

ABOVE *A fresh-looking
fabric livens up a traditional
frilled valance.*

PIPED DAY BED COVER

Fitted bedcovers are not difficult to make, provided care is taken to measure up accurately and to stitch and trim corner seams neatly so they will lie perfectly flat. This bedcover is cut short at the sides in order not to hide a beautifully turned set of legs. The lined skirt is made in four sections left open at the corners to allow the top and bottom ends to be tucked under the mattress. A pair of matching covers turn pillows into comfortable armrests by day and are easily substituted by conventional pillowcases when the bed is in use.

Sturdy furnishing fabrics, such as rep or linen union, are the best choice for a bed that doubles up as seating.

Making the fitted cover
Measure the bed as shown in the instructions for measuring a fitted divan cover (see MEASURING UP) and cut out the top fabric pieces and skirt lining accordingly. Prepare the piping to fit around the welt at the top and bottom edges (see PIPING).

Next round off each corner of the centre panel, using a saucer as a template (**1**), and trim the excess fabric around the curves down to the seam allowance.

Join the short edges of the welt to make a continuous strip, then press the seams open and attach the piping to the outside edges (see PIPING).

With right sides together and matching the welt seams with the centre panel corners, pin, tack and machine stitch all round. Notch the curved edges and press the seam up towards the welt (**2**).

2

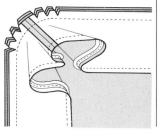

3

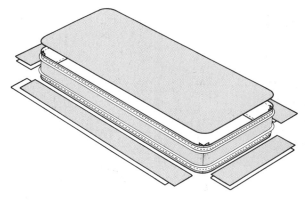

With right sides together and raw edges even, pin the lining to each skirt section and tack and stitch along three sides, leaving one long edge open. Turn right side out and press, then tack the raw edges together along each unseamed side.

Join the skirt to the welt section by section (**3**). Oversew the seams together to neaten and press them upwards. Press the finished cover and place over the day bed easing it to fit.

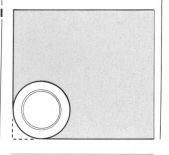

ABOVE *A sleek tailored
cover sharply defined with
contrasting piping makes the
most of a classically simple
day bed.*

DUVET COVER AND PILLOWCASE

Duvet covers and pillowcases are very easy to sew and can be embellished with trimmings and lace or picot edgings.

The most practical choice of fabric for a duvet cover is cotton sheeting, which comes in very wide widths – 178cm (70in), 228cm (90in), 264cm (104in), 275cm (108in) – but some dress fabrics can also be used. Join side strips to a centre panel when making a duvet cover out of narrow-width fabric and use a patterned fabric or trimming to disguise the seams. Match patterned fabric across joins.

Covers should fit loosely around a duvet without compressing the filling and have a generous opening to make them easy to slip on and off. Press fastener tape makes a strong closing and is easy to apply.

Making the duvet cover
Duvet covers usually come in a range of standard sizes: single 140cm × 200cm (54in × 78in), double 200cm × 200cm (78in × 78in), and king size 230cm × 220cm (90in × 86in). Select the appropriate size for your duvet and cut two pieces of fabric to fit, allowing a seam of 1.5cm ($\frac{5}{8}$in) on three sides and an 8cm (3in) hem along the base opening edges.

Turn under the opening edge of each piece to form a double 2.5cm (1in) wide hem. Pin, tack and stitch the hems.

With right sides of the fabric pieces together, pin, tack and stitch together alongside the hem for

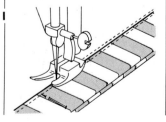

30cm (12in) in from each side for a double and king size duvet, leaving a central opening (**1**); stitch 15cm (6in) in from each side for a single. Tack the strips of fastening tape to the right side of each opening edge so that the press studs correspond (**2**), then stitch down the long edges of tape.
Use a zipper foot attachment when stitching fastener tape in place.

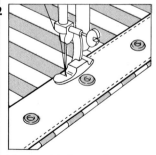

Next, with hem edges matching, stitch across the hem either side of the opening to enclose the raw edges of the fastener tape (**3**). Turn the duvet right side out.

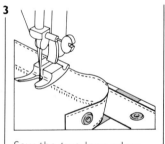

Sew the two long edges of the cover together with French seams, then join the top edges in the same way.

Making the pillowcase
The standard size of a pillowcase is 75cm × 50cm (30in × 20in). Cut a strip of fabric that measures double the length plus 26cm (10in) and add 3cm (1$\frac{1}{4}$in) to the width to allow for 1.5cm ($\frac{5}{8}$in) seams on each side.

Turn under one short edge 6.5cm (2$\frac{1}{2}$in). Then turn under the raw edge for 6mm ($\frac{1}{4}$in); pin and stitch in place through all thicknesses.

Turn under a double hem of 6mm ($\frac{1}{4}$in) along

the opposite short edge. Pin, tack and stitch. Make a flap by folding up this hem edge for 18cm (7in); press.

Fold the fabric in half widthways, wrong sides together, so the edge with the wide hem is level with the fold of the flap (**4**). Sew the side edges together with French seams.

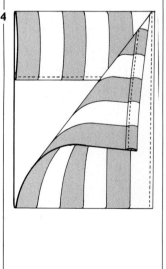

DUVET COVER AND PILLOWCASE

MUSLIN CANOPY

This muslin canopy is suspended 120cm to 150cm (4–5ft) above the bed. The purchased hoop should be approximately 60cm (24in) in diameter and the muslin should be at least 140cm (54in) in width if the canopy is to hang over a double bed. The hook from which to suspend the canopy is driven in through a ceiling joist. Decide where you want the canopy to hang in relation to the bed and position the hook accordingly.

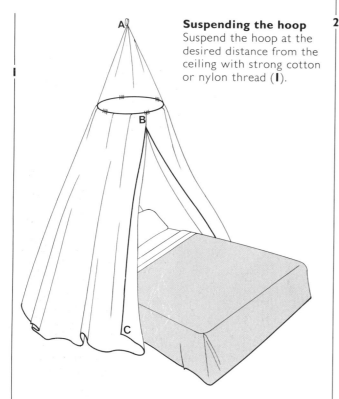

Suspending the hoop
Suspend the hoop at the desired distance from the ceiling with strong cotton or nylon thread (**1**).

Cutting the fabric
Measure the fall of the canopy **A–B–C**. Then measure the width of the canopy along the top of the bed and as far down the sides as you want the canopy to come. To ensure a generous fit, make this measurement along the floor about 10cm (4in) from the made-up bed.

The canopy consists of a centre panel and two side strips cut to measure the required width when sewn together. Allow 1cm (⅜in) for seams or turnings on all long edges. The length of the panel and side strips should equal the fall distance of the canopy (**A–B–C**) plus 30cm (12in) for draping.

Making the canopy
Join the strips to the centre panel with French seams, taking a 6mm (¼in) allowance on the first seam; trim down and stitch again taking a 6mm (¼in) allowance. Add a hem allowance of 2cm (¾in) to the **A–B** measurement and join the strip edges for this distance with a French seam as before (**2**).

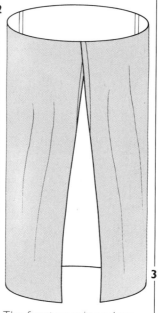

The front opening edges will now turn outwards so clip 1cm (⅜in) into the fabric just below the French seam and turn under the edges twice and hem in place.

Turn the muslin tube inside out and lay the top section flat with the front opening centred; mark the level where the opening begins at each side fold with a pin.

Draw a diagonal line from each mark to the hem foldline; the diagonals should end 8cm (3in) from the centre seam (**3**).

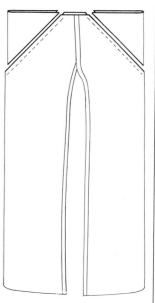

Stitch along these lines and then cut away the excess fabric, leaving a 1.5cm (⅝in) seam allowance. Trim down the raw edge on one side of the seam to 6mm (¼in) and fold over the untrimmed edge to make a self-bound seam (**4**).

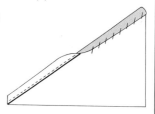

Turn the tube right side out and press under a double hem of 1cm (⅜in) along the top edge. Run two rows of gathering stitches along this hem. Cut a 6cm (2½in) length of 2cm (¾in) wide tape and press under the ends.

Positioning the canopy
Position in place over the hoop and draw up the gathering stitches. Make

sure the centre front opening is positioned at the centre front of the hoop. Secure the gathering and stitch each end of the tape to either side of the gathered section to make a loop. Slip the loop over the hook and oversew the hoop to the canopy (**5**).

4

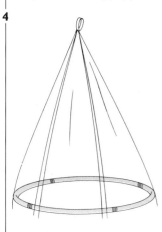

Trim any excess fabric at the base edge, curving the fabric if necessary. Turn under a double 6mm ($\frac{1}{4}$in) hem and stitch.

RIGHT *This fantasy canopy has been made up in undyed muslin. A devastating effect can be achieved by dipping the muslin in different dyes section by section to produce soft rainbow hues.*

TRADITIONAL FUTON

A futon is a firm mattress made up of layers of flock wadding encased in a strong cotton fabric which is tie-quilted with twine. Used on the floor, or supported on a slatted wood base, the futon can be rolled up to make a giant backrest by day or packed away out of sight when you need the space.

As the widths of wadding available to the home sewer are usually narrow, they need to be joined if you want a futon wider than single bed size. The joins should be staggered layer by layer to avoid a lump running the length of the futon. You will need an upholsterer's needle and twine to secure the layers of wadding.

Cutting out the wadding and cover fabric

Decide what width futon you would like. It should be approximately 190cm (75in) long, up to 10cm (4in) deep and be filled with layers of 2.5cm (1in) thick wadding. Fabric widths needed to cover a futon width of 75cm (30in), 90cm (36in) or 120cm (48in) are: 90cm (36in), 120cm (48in) and 140cm (54in) respectively.

The futon cover is a large bag made from two pieces of fabric joined together lengthways down the centre front and back and across each end (**1**). Calculate the fabric cutting size as follows. To the width measurement add the desired depth of the futon plus a seam allowance of 4cm (1⅝in). To the length measurement add the depth plus a seam allowance of 3cm (1¼in). Cut two pieces of fabric to these dimensions.

Cut the layers of wadding to the length dimension. If widths are to be joined, cut them so they can be staggered as shown (**4**). There is no need to include a seam allowance when calculating the wadding.

Making the futon cover

To form the back opening through which the wadding is stuffed, press in one long edge of one of the fabric pieces by 2.5cm (1in) and then open out. With right sides together and raw edges even, pin, tack and stitch the fabric pieces together for 15cm (6in) at either end, taking a 1.5cm (⅝in) seam allowance.

Fold the seam to one side along the previously pressed crease and press.

Next join the fabric pieces down the centre front and across the top and bottom ends to make a bag, taking seam allowances of 1.5cm (⅝in). Zigzag stitch the seam allowances together (**2**).

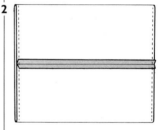

To make the corners of the bag, stitch evenly across each corner through both thicknesses of fabric (**3**), the length of the stitching should correspond to the depth of the futon. Trim the

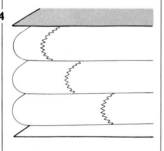

corners and zigzag stitch the seam allowances together, then press all seams and turn the futon cover to the right side.

Mark the positions of the ties on top and bottom.

Join the widths of wadding if necessary (see WADDINGS for joining instructions), staggering the joins (**4**). Then place the sheets of wadding on top of each other and stitch very loosely together with lines of diagonal tacking.

Insert the wadding smoothly and evenly and then slip hem across the opening using a double thickness of thread.

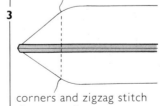

Thread the upholstery needle with a double or quadruple length of twine and, leaving loose ends of 10cm (4in), take the needle through to the back of the futon 12mm (½in) to the side of the tie position. Take a 2.5cm (1in) stitch sideways and bring the needle through to the top again. Tie the ends of twine in a firm reef knot (see KNOTS) and trim to 6.5cm (2½in) (**5**). Continue until all the quilting has been completed.

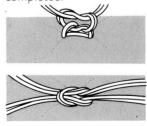

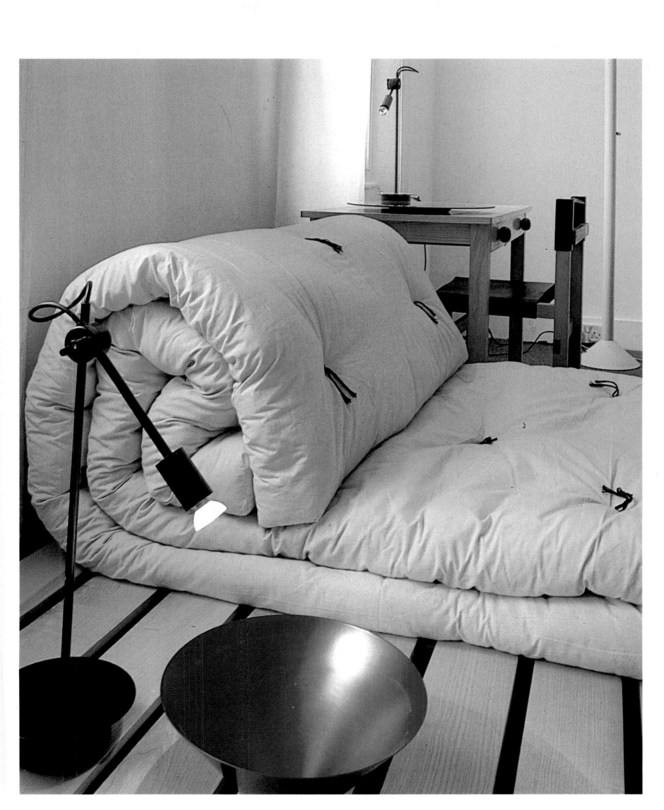

ABOVE *Japanese in origin,
the futon has become
popular in the West as an
alternative sleeping
arrangement.*

187

LEAF MOTIF QUILT

This lightweight quilt can provide year-round bedding in warmer climates and well-heated homes. As large-scale quilting is almost impossible on a domestic sewing machine, the wadding used for each leaf design is cut out and attached separately to the top fabric and the main wadding is machine stitched to the lining and then sewn by hand to the inner and outer points of the leaves. The picot edging can be machine made or hand worked.

The quilt is made from wide-width sheeting, so there is no need for fabric joins, and a synthetic filling makes it fully washable. Use a lightweight layer of fabric such as muslin as a backing for the leaves.

RIGHT *Luxurious but functional, this exquisite quilt is much easier to make than it looks.*

Making the quilt
Measure the length and width of the mattress and allow a 30cm (12in) overhang all round plus a seam allowance of 2cm ($\frac{3}{4}$in) on each side. Cut equal-sized pieces of top and backing fabric, wadding and lining.

Trace the leaf motif (far right) on to graph paper, scaling it up to the desired size. Cut out the leaf from A to B, fold over and draw round the shape. Cut along this outline to obtain a complete leaf. Using this as a template, cut out 16 leaf shapes from extra wadding, and three more from paper.

Group four templates on the right side of the

top fabric at each corner, pivoting each one as shown (**1**). Pin in place and tack around each shape so that the leaves are outlined on the cloth.

Pin each wadding shape against the stitched outline on the back of the fabric and tack in position. Next tack the top and backing fabric together down the length, across the width and along the sides. Topstitch around each leaf shape through all layers (**2**) just inside the tacked outline to quilt the leaves.

2

Lay the main wadding on the wrong side of the lining fabric and tack loosely in place across the middle both ways and around the edges. Stitch the layers together along the

seamlines and trim the wadding to within 6mm ($\frac{1}{4}$in) of the stitching line on all sides.

Making the edging
Cut four 13cm (5$\frac{1}{4}$in) wide strips of fabric equal in length and width to the edges of the quilt plus 13cm (5$\frac{1}{4}$in). Press the strips in half lengthways. Join them at the corners in the same way as for the CO-ORDINATED TABLECLOTH border, but do not press under the edges.

Trace the edging outline (far right) on to cardboard and cut out a template. Lay it along one side of the edging rectangle with the points barely touching the folded edge and draw round the template until each side has been marked. Stitch just inside the outline to make a firm edge. Next zigzag stitch over the outline to produce a close satin stitch (see CUTWORK TABLECLOTH), and trim off the excess fabric (**3**). Otherwise embroider by hand (see EMBROIDERY).

3

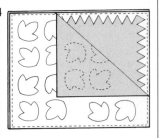

With the right side of the lining facing and raw edges even (**4**), pin and tack the edging to the lining through all thicknesses, taking a 1.5cm ($\frac{5}{8}$in) seam allowance. Join the lining and quilt as shown in the instructions for the QUILTED BEDCOVER.

4

Bringing the needle from the back of the quilt, hand stitch all the layers together at the inner and outer points of each leaf.

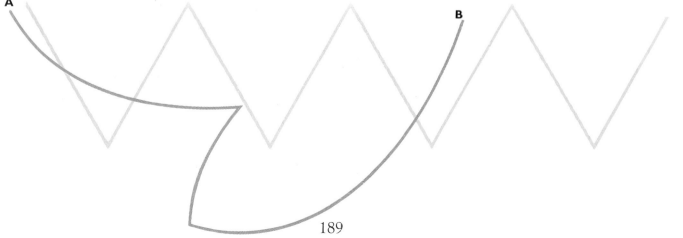

A

B

189

FOUR PILLOWCASES

Pillowcase with ties

For the pillowcase cut out one piece of fabric 153cm by 53cm (60¼in by 21in). For the facing cut out two pieces each 53cm by 11.5cm (21in by 4½in). For the ties cut out six pieces each 28cm by 3cm (11in by 1¼in).

Fold each tie piece in half lengthways with wrong sides together and tuck in 1cm (⅜in) at one end and along the length. Pin, tack and topstitch.

Fold the pillowcase piece in half widthways with right sides together. Pin, tack and stitch the sides, taking a 1.5cm (⅝in) seam allowance. Trim and zigzag stitch the raw edges together to neaten. Turn to right side.

Position the ties in pairs to the right side of the pillowcase edge, with the first pairs 10cm (4in) from the side edges and the remaining pair centrally in between. Pin and tack in place.

Place the facing pieces one on top of the other, right sides together. Pin, tack and stitch across the short edges to make a ring, taking a 1.5cm (⅝in) seam allowance.

With raw edges even, place the right side of the facing to the top edge of pillowcase over the ties, matching side seams. Pin, tack and stitch the facing to the pillowcase. Trim the seams and turn the facing to the inside. Turn under the raw edge for 5cm (2in). Pin, tack and topstitch in place all round the pillowcase.

Lace-edged pillowcase

Cut out one piece of fabric 175cm by 53cm (69in by 21in) for the pillowcase. On one short edge turn under a double 6mm (¼in) hem. Pin, tack and stitch. On the opposite short edge turn under a double 5cm (2in) hem; pin, tack and stitch the hem in place.

Cut one length of 6.5cm (2½in) wide lace edging equal to the width of the pillowcase. Place to the right side of the fabric, just overlapping the wide hemmed edge. Pin, tack and topstitch the lace in place. Cut a second length and, overlapping the first length, pin, tack and topstitch in place.

Mark across the pillowcase 15cm (6in) from the narrow hemmed edge. Fold the pillowcase with right sides together so that the lace-hemmed edge is level with this mark. Turn down the narrow hemmed edge to make a 15cm (6in) flap. Pin, tack and stitch the side edges of the pillowcase, then trim and zigzag stitch the raw edges together to neaten. Turn the pillowcase to the right side.

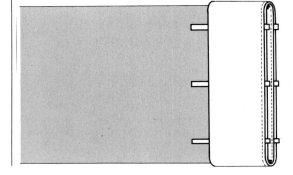

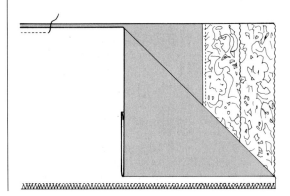

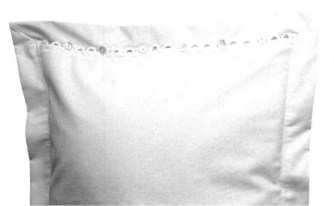

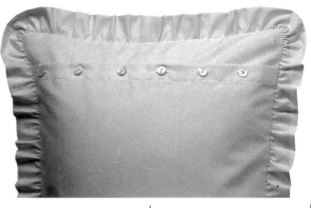

Rouleau-edged pillowcase

For the front cut out one piece of fabric 98cm by 76cm (38½in by 30in). For the back cut out one piece 78cm by 53cm (30¾in by 21in). For the facing cut out one piece 53cm by 4cm (21in by 1½in).

Make up a 60cm (24in) rouleau strip (see ROULEAU). Place 2cm (¾in) wide loops along one short edge of the back, so they will protrude just 12mm (½in) beyond the edge when it has been faced. Place the facing against the back edge with right sides together. Pin tack and stitch, taking a 1.5cm (⅝in) seam allowance. Turn the facing over to the wrong side of the pillowcase and press under the raw edge

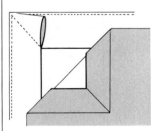

to meet the stitching. Pin, tack and stitch.

On the front turn 6.5cm

(2½in) to the right side. At each corner, pin the excess fabric into a dart.

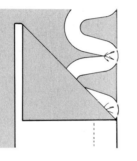

Trim off the fabric to 1.5cm (⅝in) and stitch the darts to within 1.5cm (⅝in) of the inner edges. Trim and turn the border to the wrong side. Press under 1.5cm (⅝in) all round the border edge. Position the pillowcase back to the front with wrong sides together, tucking the back seam allowance under the border edge.

Pin, tack and stitch around the border close to the folded edge. Stitch round the border again 6mm (¼in) from the first row of stitching. Stitch six evenly spaced 1.5cm (⅝in) diameter buttons along the border edge, to match up with a rouleau loop.

Frilled pillowcase

For the front cut one piece of fabric 78cm by 53cm (30½in by 21in). For the back cut out one piece 75.5cm by 53cm (29¾in by 21in) and one piece 14cm by 53cm (5½in by 21in). For the frill measure around the pillowcase front and make up one length of fabric to double this distance by 13cm (5in).

Pin, tack and stitch the frill together into a ring. Fold the frill in half with wrong sides together. Gather and tack to the pillowcase front (see FRILLS).

On one short edge of the larger back piece turn under a double 3cm (1¼in) hem; pin, tack and stitch. Repeat on one long edge of the smaller back piece. Overlap the pieces (larger

over smaller) by the hem width. Pin and tack together at the side edges. Mark six evenly spaced buttonholes down the larger piece. Mark through the fabric for the positions of 1.5cm (⅝in) diameter buttons. Separate the fabric pieces and work a buttonhole at each position. Stitch on a button at each position on the smaller piece. Overlap the hemmed edges together as before and pin.

With the right sides together, and raw edges even, position the combined back pieces against the front over the frill. Pin, tack and stitch together all round, taking a 1.5cm (⅝in) seam allowance. Zigzag stitch the raw edges together to neaten.

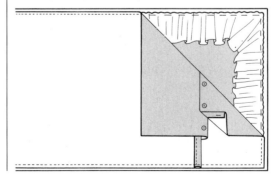

BASIC TECHNIQUES

FABRIC FILE

ADVICE ON FABRIC SELECTION

Personal taste and aesthetic considerations aside, the criteria for choosing a particular furnishing fabric are: the suitability of the weight and weave for a particular type of furnishing; its ability to withstand the effects of everyday wear and tear. These obviously vary in intensity from home to home.

The following checklist can be worked through when you have tracked down a fabric that you find appealing and are considering whether to buy.
1. Roll out a length of the fabric in the shop to see what effect would be created when covering a large area in your home. Ask to look at it in daylight.
2. Gather up a length to assess how well the fabric drapes for curtains; crumple a section in your hand to see if it creases too much to be a satisfactory choice for loose covers. Is it heavy enough to cover the bristly pile of an old sofa or chairs? Is it too fine to be used for blinds?
3. If in any doubt whether the fabric is the correct weave or weight, find someone qualified to advise you – even if it means going to another shop.
4. Examine the cut edge of the fabric to see whether it frays or whether pieces of pile detach themselves easily. Be prepared to deal with the problem if you buy fabric that frays.
5. Watch carefully for flaws as the fabric is measured and point them out to the assistant. You should be given additional fabric to compensate for any flawed pieces. This is especially important when making curtains as it is usually impossible to cut around flaws.
6. Check what the fabric is made of, its shrink- and stain-resistant properties, and whether it should be machine washed or dry cleaned. Pale unpatterned fabrics or the presence of a sticky-fingered toddler would make machine-washable fabric a practical choice.
7. Buy enough fabric to complete your furnishing project. Otherwise, if you do have to return to the shop for an extra length, you may find there is a new batch in stock with a noticeable variation in colour.

A TO Z OF FURNISHING FABRICS

Brocade
A crisp satin-weave fabric with a raised floral design that gives an embroidered look. Cotton and synthetic blends now make brocade a more practical longer lasting choice for furnishings than the original silk and, in medium to heavy weights, it can be used for curtains, cushions and some upholstery. It frays easily so hems should be doubled and seams bound.

Broderie Anglaise
Fine self-coloured cotton or cotton/polyester fabric, usually white, with an all-over embroidered eyelet design. Suitable for sheer curtains and also available as an edging, sometimes pre-gathered, for frilled cushions, blinds, cot bumpers and so on.

Buckram
A stiffening fabric that is used as a backing for tie-backs and pelmets. It is made from coarse cotton impregnated with size for greater rigidity.

As it is very stiff and springy it may be necessary to place objects on the corners to hold it down while cutting out. Do not add seam allowances as it is too stiff to include in seams. It will not fray.

Calico
Firmly woven, strong cotton fabric, plain or printed, that washes and wears well, although it tends to crease. Unbleached calico is often used for mattress covers.

Canvas
A sturdy, coarse cotton fabric sometimes known as 'duck' and used mainly for covering garden chairs and awnings. Very hard to sew.

Chintz
A traditional furnishing fabric made from close-weave cotton and usually overprinted with large-scale patterns of birds and flowers. Glazed chintz has a resin coating which gives the fabric its characteristic sheen; this coating is permanent and dust and dirt shedding.

Corduroy
An inexpensive plain-weave cotton fabric with a ribbed pile effect, available in different widths from the large 'jumbo' or 'elephant' cord to the finest needlecord. It can be used for upholstery, but with regular heavy use it will crease and the pile will flatten. Needlecord should be limited to curtains.

To avoid shading, pieces should be cut with the pile running upwards. Corduroy will fray, as the pile detaches easily, so finish raw edges.

Cretonne
A hard-wearing fabric made from printed or plain cotton similar in appearance to unglazed chintz. Being washable, it is a practical choice for most soft furnishings. Allow for shrinkage.

Damask
Self-coloured satiny fabric with traditional floral designs woven into the surface. Originally made in silk but now available in a variety of fibres and blends, including linen, which is most popular for tablecloths and napkins.

Denim
The original twill-weave cotton overall cloth may be used for inexpensive furnishings, particularly loose covers, although its stiffness makes it difficult to sew. It softens with wear, but beware of the characteristic fading that is the result of regular washing.

Domette
A soft interlining fabric made from cotton or cotton blends used mainly where a padded effect is required and to give greater insulation to lined curtains.

Gabardine
A lightweight closely woven fabric with a prominent diagonal rib. It is hard-

194

wearing and water-repellent but frays easily.

Gauze

Loosely woven plain-weave fabric, generally made from cotton, and suitable for sheer curtains.

Gingham

A firm cotton or cotton/polyester cloth with interwoven stripes or checks in a variety of colours with white. It is generally used in dressmaking, but is suitable for light curtains and table linen.

Hessian

A coarse, loosely woven cloth made from jute, or jute with hemp, that is used for wallcoverings and noticeboards and, if pre-shrunk, can make inexpensive curtains and blinds. Hessian frays easily.

Holland

Firm, hard-wearing, plain-weave fabric made from cotton or linen and often stiffened with size or oil, which makes it suitable for blinds as well as upholstery undercovering.

Lace

Originally made by hand in linen, modern lace is usually produced by machine from nylon, viscose or cotton. An open-work fabric in a variety of designs, it is available in wide widths for sheer curtains, pre-finished panels for door or café curtains, and narrow widths as a flat or gathered trimming.

Lawn

A fine smooth fabric made from cotton blends with a slightly crisp finish. Hem by hand.

Linen

Thick, loosely woven fabric made from natural flax fibres and used extensively for table dressings. It is often blended with cotton to make hard-wearing upholstery fabric.

Moiré

The term that refers to a water-mark finish applied to a variety of furnishing fabrics, including cotton, satin and taffeta.

Net

A transparent curtain fabric made from cotton or synthetic yarns knotted together to form a mesh. It will not fray when cut and raw edges do not have to be neatened.

Rep(p)

A stiff medium- to heavyweight fabric with a pronounced rib made from a variety of fibres, particularly cotton or a cotton blend. It is especially hard-wearing and an excellent choice for upholstery and loose covers.

Make sure all the ribs are running in the same direction when cutting out. It tends to fray, so handle carefully after cutting. Seams should be neatened

Sateen

A soft cotton fabric with a slight surface sheen that is made in plain colours and a variety of weights, from fine lining to heavier curtaining.

Satin

As sateen, but with a more pronounced sheen on the right side, cotton satin is a hard-wearing choice for curtains, bedcovers and upholstery.

Seersucker

Cotton/polyester or nylon fabric crinkled during manufacture to give a permanent bubble effect. For usage see Gingham.

Shantung

Originally a slubbed Chinese silk using yarn of irregular thickness to produce an uneven textured surface. Now made from cotton and man-made fibres, it is suitable for most soft furnishings. Seams should be neatened.

Taffeta

A crisp plain-weave fabric with a distinct sheen made from various blends of synthetic fibres. Its use in furnishing is best limited to lampshades and cushions. Most types of taffeta fray.

Ticking

A robust cotton twill closely woven in narrow stripes that are traditionally black and white. It is mainly used for pillow and mattress covers, but can be used for upholstery, although it is very hard to sew. Neaten raw edges inside covers if they are to be removed for washing.

Tweed

Coarsely woven fabric with a hand-loomed look, often in wool. The loose texture makes it unsuitable for seat covers, but it works well for curtains, being both warm and flame-resistant.

Twill

A distinct diagonal weave that can be applied to a variety of tough hard-wearing fabrics.

Velvet

Furnishing velvet is made from cotton or man-made fibres (or a combination of the two) with a closely woven backing and cut pile surface (deep pile is referred to as 'plush'). It is difficult to handle and should be avoided by the beginner. Most velvets need to be dry cleaned.

Always cut the fabric pieces so that the direction of the pile will give a rich dark effect when the pieces are made up. Apply pattern pieces to the wrong side of the folded velvet and outline lightly with tailor's chalk. Cut out each piece singly if the pile catches, placing the pattern on the wrong side of the cloth.

Tack and machine all seams in the direction of the pile otherwise puckering results.

Velveteen

Similar to velvet, although easier to sew, velveteen is usually made from cotton with a pile running across the weave. It wears and presses well.

Voile

A fine lightweight fabric made from a variety of yarns including cotton. Plain or patterned, it is ideal for sheer curtains as it drapes well.

Wadding

Cotton or polyester padding, resembling cotton wool, that is enclosed in sheets of thin paper-like covering. In various depths and weights, it is used in re-upholstery and quilting.

WADDINGS AND LININGS

WADDINGS

Wadding comes in three weights: light (50g/2oz), medium (100g/4oz), and heavy (200g/8oz). The first weight is used to pad appliqué shapes, the other two are used in re-upholstery and quilting. Flock wadding, which is thicker and denser, is available from upholsterers and specialist dealers. The widest wadding width available is 95cm (37in).

If sheets of wadding have to be joined to gain a wider width, pull the edge of one sheet slightly over the other and join the two sheets with herringbone stitch. Wadding can also be used in layers if greater thickness/weight is required.

LININGS

All curtains are improved by a lining, either fixed or detachable. A lining makes the curtains hang better, protects the fabric from light and dirt and helps insulate the room and reduce noise. Choose the best lining fabric you can afford as a poor lining will wear out long before the curtains.

Cotton sateen is the most common lining fabric. It is available in two widths – 120cm (48in) and 137cm (54in) – and is sold in a range of colours as well as neutral shades, which are usually cheaper.

Also available is thermal lining: either a cotton/acrylic fabric in white or beige, or the more common and expensive aluminium-coated lining that reflects heat in summer and prevents it from escaping in winter.

Black-out lining comes in neutral shades, not black as the name suggests. As well as excluding all light, this type of lining also possesses thermal qualities.

See LINED CURTAINS for instructions on attaching a fixed lining. Detachable linings are made up separately in the same way as an unlined curtain. Special heading tape for detachable linings enables you to hang the lining on the same hook as the curtain.

Interlining

Interlining refers to the extra layer that can be stitched between the curtain fabric and the lining. As well as giving the curtain a professional finish – the best – it will give added insulation.

Interlining comes in a variety of thicknesses. Choose the one that is most appropriate for your curtain fabric.

Bump is the thickest and looks like a fleecy blanket. Domette is a brushed cotton and the most commonly used interlining. The thinnest is a bonded synthetic fibre. Most interlining is 120cm (48in) wide and either white or off-white in colour.

To match a wide curtain width, overlap the long edges of the interlining widths and herringbone stitch them together rather than join them with ordinary seams. On thick fabrics this stitching is worked on both sides.

Once interlined, the curtains will have to be dry cleaned, as interlining will not wash successfully.

INTERFACINGS

Some soft furnishings must be stiffened in parts, or throughout, in order to achieve the right shape.

There are four categories of interfacing: woven sew-in, woven iron-on, non-woven sew-in and non-woven iron-on. Before you buy any interfacing, make sure that is the right weight for your fabric. Avoid choosing one that makes the fabric look too stiff. Also make sure the interfacing can be cleaned in the same way as your fabric.

Woven interfacing

This category includes sheer fabrics, soft translucent cotton and linen canvas. Some have an adhesive on one side so they can be ironed on to the fabric. Woven interfacing must be cut following the grain.

Non-woven interfacing

Non-woven interfacing is made from fibres fused together with a bonding agent. It can be cut with the pattern pieces lying in any direction. This type of interfacing comes in a wide range of weights in both sew-in and iron-on varieties.

Applying iron-on interfacing

Trim away the seam allowances of the interfacing unless it is very light.

Place the interfacing sticky side down on the right side of the fabric, within the seamlines. Using a dry iron on a warm setting, press the interfacing in place. Do not slide the iron across the fabric.

Applying sew-in interfacing

Light- to mediumweight interfacing may be included in the fabric seams. Apply the interfacing to the wrong side of the fabric and tack in place close to the seamline. Stitch the fabric sections together in the usual way and then trim the interfacing to about 6mm ($\frac{1}{4}$in).

Firm and heavyweight interfacings are applied within the seamlines. Trim the seam allowances from the interfacing. Place it so that it lies just inside the seamlines and on the wrong side of the fabric; tack in place.

Herringbone stitch the interfacing to the seam allowance around the edges. Take care not to trim away these stitches when trimming seams.

MACHINE QUILTING

Using a quilting guide attachment

This is the simplest aid to making regularly spaced lines of quilting stitches and reduces marking out to a minimum, as once the first line of a design is marked and providing the following lines are parallel, you can stitch from this first line without any marking. Follow the maker's instructions when attaching the guide.

STITCHES

Backstitch

Commonly called imitation machine stitch, backstitch will hold fabric pieces firmly together even though it is worked by hand.

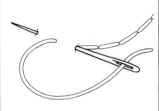

Bring the needle and thread through to the upper side of the fabric. Insert the needle about 3mm ($\frac{1}{8}$in) behind the point where the thread came out. Bring the needle forward and out the same distance in front of that point. Continue inserting and bringing up the needle a stitch length behind and in front of the previous stitch. Stitches on the underside will be twice as long as those on the upper side.

Blanket stitch

Worked by hand, this stitch is used to neaten raw edges or as a decoration.

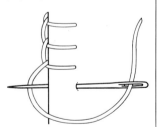

Fasten the working thread just under the fabric edge and then insert the needle down through the fabric at the desired distance inwards. The needle should be at right angles to the edge. Holding the working thread under the needle point, pull through.

Buttonhole stitch

This is used for neatening buttonholes and for stitching hooks and eyes and press fasteners firmly in place.

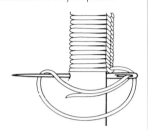

Working in the opposite direction to blanket stitch, insert the needle upwards through the fabric at the desired distance from the edge and twist the working thread around the point. Pull the needle through, bringing the knot thus formed to the raw edge.

Gathering

see RUNNING STITCH

Hemming stitch

Use this stitch when sewing a hem in place by hand.

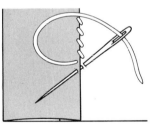

Fasten the working thread inside the hem. Then make small slanting stitches through the fabric and the hem in one movement. Pick up one or two threads of fabric with each stitch and space the stitches evenly across the hem.

Herringbone stitch

This stitch is used to hold hems firmly in place. Work

from left to right with the folded hem edge facing towards you.

Fasten the working thread and bring it up through the hem 3mm ($\frac{1}{8}$in) from the edge. Move 6mm ($\frac{1}{4}$in) diagonally to the right and take a 3mm ($\frac{1}{8}$in) long stitch from right to left just above the hem edge.

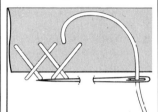

Move 6mm ($\frac{1}{4}$in) diagonally up to the right and take a 3mm ($\frac{1}{8}$in) stitch from right to left. Bring the needle diagonally down again and repeat, making crossed stitches along the hem edge.

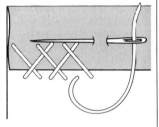

Ladder stitch

When joining two pieces of patterned fabric, the pattern must be matched across the seam and this is achieved by tacking together the fabric pieces from the right side.

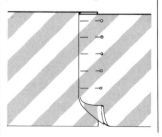

Press under the seam allowance along one edge and place over the seam allowance of the other so that the pattern matches exactly. Pin firmly in place.

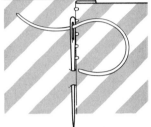

Make a knot under the folded edge and take the needle across the join into the flat piece of fabric. Take it under the fabric, along the seamline, for about 2cm ($\frac{3}{4}$in) and then pull through and take a stitch across the join

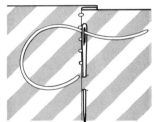

into the folded edge again, between the two layers of fabric.

Take a stitch of about 2cm ($\frac{3}{4}$in) and bring up the needle. Take another stitch across the join.

Continue in this way along the seam, forming straight ladder-like stitches. When complete the two pieces can be folded with right sides together ready for stitching.

Lockstitch

Used in curtain making to hold the lining and interlining loosely to the curtain fabric.

Place the lining over the curtain fabric with wrong sides together. Pin the centres together down the complete length. Fold the lining back against the pins.

Working with a thread that matches the curtain fabric and at right angles to the folded edge, take a stitch through the folded edge and curtain fabric, picking up only one or two threads of fabric with each stitch. Make the next stitch about 5cm (2in) to the right, taking the needle over the working thread, thus producing loops of thread.

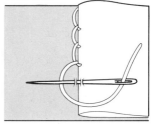

Work the length of the fold, keeping the stitches very loose. Work additional lockstitch rows as required, working two or three rows to every 120cm (48in) width.

Oversewing
This stitch is used mainly for neatening raw edges by hand.

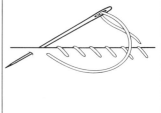

Secure the thread on the wrong side. Working from left to right, take the needle diagonally over the edge and through the fabric about 3mm to 6mm ($\frac{1}{8}$in–$\frac{1}{4}$in) from the starting point and 3mm ($\frac{1}{8}$in) down from the edge. Repeat to the end, taking care not to pull the stitches too tight as this will make the edge curl.

Use longer stitches on bulky fabric, deeper ones on fabric that frays easily.

Prickstitch
This is worked in the same way as backstitch, but the top stitches are smaller and should appear as pricks in the surface of the fabric.

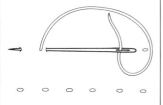

When taking a stitch backwards insert the needle one or two fabric threads behind where the thread came out. Then take a stitch 6mm ($\frac{1}{4}$in) in front of that point. Repeat from the beginning.

Running stitch
A hand-worked stitch used mainly for gathering. As it is a weak stitch it is not recommended for seams, and backstitch should be used if a seam is too awkwardly placed to be sewn by machine.

To sew a single running stitch, begin with a backstitch to hold the working thread then make small evenly spaced stitches along the fabric. Finish with another backstitch.

When used for gathering, work two rows 6mm ($\frac{1}{4}$in) apart on either side of the seamline, leaving the threads dangling at one end. Then gently slide the fabric along the threads from this end until the fabric is evenly gathered.

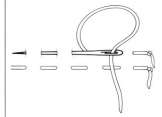

Secure the threads by twisting in a figure eight around a pin. Adjust the gathering to the required amount.

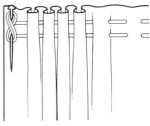

Slip hemming
This stitch is used not only to hold hems in place nearly invisibly on both sides of the fabric but also to stitch down any other folded edge.

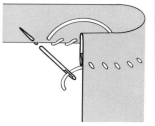

Turn under the hem and raw edge for the appropriate amount and tack in place. Working from right to left with the folded hem edge

towards you, take a tiny stitch in the main fabric close to the hem. Without pulling the thread through, slip the needle into the folded edge as close as possible to the first stitch and bring it out about 6mm ($\frac{1}{4}$in) to the left. Make these stitches in one movement. Then pull the thread through.

Continue taking stitches about 6mm ($\frac{1}{4}$in) apart.

Slipstitch
This stitch is used to join two folded edges together.

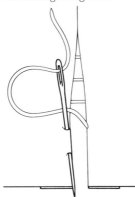

Fasten the thread inside one folded edge then cross over the opening into the opposite fold. Make a stitch about 6mm ($\frac{1}{4}$in) long and pull the needle through into the other fold again.

Repeat, working backwards and forwards across the gap and inserting the needle slightly to the inside of the fold. The stitches should be invisible.

Tacking
A long running stitch, tacking can be worked quickly by machine or hand and holds two or more pieces of fabric in position, ready for final stitching. When tacking delicate fabrics, use a fine thread that

will not mark the cloth.

Begin hand tacking with a knot so that stitches are easy to remove. Simply cut off the knot and pull the thread through the fabric from the other end.

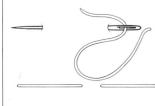

To remove machine stitches cut the top thread at intervals along the seamline and pull out with the bobbin thread from the wrong side.

Tailor's tacks

These stitches are used to transfer pattern markings on to fabric. They do not leave a mark that may be difficult to remove as other marking-up methods may do.

Use ordinary sewing thread in a colour that contrasts with the fabric. If several types of mark are required on one piece use different coloured threads to distinguish them. Use a double strand of thread about 48cm (18in) long.

Take a small loose stitch in the point to be marked, leaving ends about 3cm (1¼in) long. Then take another small stitch in the same place leaving a loop as long as the thread ends. Cut off the

thread at the same length.

Before removing the pattern cut the loop between it and the fabric. If the fabric has been cut doubled, separate the layers slightly and clip the threads between them.

Whipstitch

This is used to join two edges by hand, patchwork for example, or to attach a trimming to a fabric edge. It is similar to oversewing, but is worked from right to left, using smaller stitches.

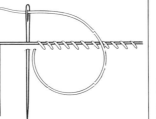

With right sides together and raw edges even, secure the working thread on the edge nearest you. Take the needle diagonally over both edges and bring it through to the front very close to the top, picking up only a few fabric threads. Work the stitches close together; there should be at least seven per centimetre (⅜in) for patchwork.

EMBROIDERY STITCHES

Overcast stitch

This stitch resembles a fine cord and is most often used in white work for stems and outlines. The small close stitches are raised slightly by first laying down a row of running stitches or by working them over one or more laid threads.

Satin stitch

This stitch is used for fillings and shaded effects. The stitches, best worked on a frame, can be of varying lengths but must lie flat and even, giving a smooth finish with precise outlines. First outline the motif with backstitch and work the satin stitch over and close to this outline. This technique gives more definition to the edge of the shape.

Bullion knotted threadwork

Secure the thread. Push the needle into the fabric but do not pull through. Wrap the thread around the point of the needle the desired amount of times.

Hold down the twisted thread, which should be coiled firmly but not tightly to enable the needle to pass through smoothly with least disturbance to the twists. Pull the needle through gently but do not pull the twisted length tight. Insert the needle into the other edge of the fabric and finish off.

Lazy daisy stitch

This is a variation of chain stitch, one of the most commonly used embroidery stitches.

Bring the needle through the fabric and insert into the same hole, thus forming a loop. Holding the loop down with the thumb, bring the needle up again through the loop a short distance away from the starting point and pull the thread through. Secure the loop with a small straight stitch. Single free-standing loops can be made by working the small straight stitch over the point where the needle enters the fabric thread instead of over the loop.

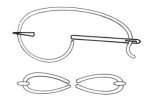

SEAMS

Plain seam

Place the fabric with right sides together, raw edges level; pin. Next tack just inside the seamline and then stitch 1.5cm ($\frac{5}{8}$in) from the raw edges.

Work a few stitches in reverse at each end of the seam to secure the threads.

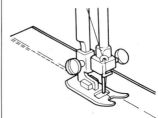

Remove the tacking stitches and press open the seam unless otherwise instructed.

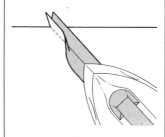

Stitching corners

To stitch a neat pointed corner raise the presser foot, leaving the needle in the fabric, and turn the fabric so that the new seamline is aligned for stitching, then lower the presser foot and continue machining. Trim the seam allowance across the point.

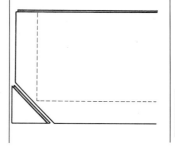

On very sharp corners stitch one, two or three stitches across the corner. The number of stitches depends on the thickness of the fabric. Trim the seam allowance around the corner.

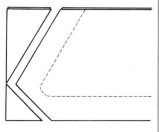

When stitching a straight gusset or piping to the corner, position the gusset seams at the corner and split open the seam or cut out a small square of fabric from the gusset or piping fabric to allow the fabric to turn the corner neatly.

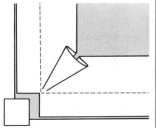

Clipping curves

After stitching curved edges clip into the seam allowance on outward curves at evenly spaced intervals. Cut evenly spaced wedge shapes from inward curves. This will allow the seam allowance to lie flat when pressed open.

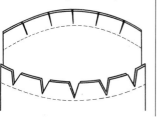

Neatening raw edges

The simplest method of neatening seam allowance edges is to zigzag stitch them on a machine. Use a short narrow stitch worked slightly in from the raw edge. If the fabric frays badly, use a large zigzag stitch worked over the raw edge. When the fabric is fine, turn under the raw edges and either zigzag or straight stitch.

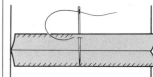

If neatening by hand, oversew the raw edges. Work from left to right, taking the stitches diagonally over the edge about 3mm ($\frac{1}{8}$in) apart. If the fabric frays, work a row of straight stitching first, then oversew the edge.

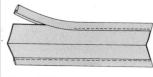

Raw edges can also be bound, together or separately, by folding binding evenly in half over the edges. Pin and stitch in place.

For self-binding, trim down one seam allowance. Then fold the wider allowance over the trimmed edge and stitch in place.

Flat fell seam

This self-neatening seam is used on home furnishings that must be frequently laundered as it is very strong. It is especially suitable for items that take a lot of strain.

Place the fabric pieces with right sides together, pin and stitch a plain seam. Press the seam allowance to one side. Trim down the underneath allowance to 6mm ($\frac{1}{4}$in). Fold the top allowance over the trimmed edge, enclosing it. Press this fold flat and pin and stitch it to the fabric close to the edge.

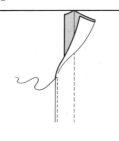

French seam

Another self-neatening seam used mainly on sheer and lightweight fabrics. A French seam can only be worked on straight edges.

Pin the two edges with wrong sides together. Tack if the fabric is slippery and then stitch 6mm ($\frac{1}{4}$in) from the raw edges.

Refold with right sides together; pin and stitch the seam again 1cm ($\frac{3}{8}$in) from the seamed edge.

HEMS

TURNING UNDER A HEM

Single hem
If the fabric is very heavy the hem should only be turned under once.

Turn under the hem for the required amount and press. Stitch close to the edge to neaten and herringbone stitch over the edge.

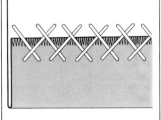

Uneven width hem
This hem is suitable for medium- to heavyweight fabrics.

Turn under the hem for the required amount and press. Then press under the raw edge by 6mm ($\frac{1}{4}$in). Pin in place and machine stitch or hem by hand.

Double hem
This is suitable for use where a firm edge is required. In the case of sheer fabrics it is essential to prevent the raw edges showing through.

Turn under the hem once for the required amount and then turn under the complete folded width again. Pin and machine stitch in place or hem by hand.

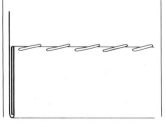

FOLDING MITRED CORNERS

To turn a hem neatly round a corner, the fabric should be folded into a mitre. The hem can be of uneven depth, as in the turnings along the sides and base of a curtain.

Single hem
Neaten the raw edges as desired and then turn under the hem along both edges of the fabric for the required amount and press. Mark each raw edge where the turnings intersect with a pin.

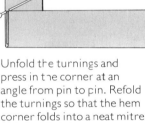

Unfold the turnings and press in the corner at an angle from pin to pin. Refold the turnings so that the hem corner folds into a neat mitre and slipstitch its edges together.

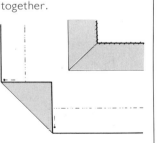

Uneven width hem
Follow the instructions given for the above, omitting the neatening. Press in the corner and then unfold again. Press under the raw edges of the hem by 6mm ($\frac{1}{4}$in) and then refold the corner and turnings to make a neat mitre. Slipstitch.

Double hem
Turn under the hem once along both edges of the fabric for the required amount and press. Double one turning and mark where it falls on the edge fold with a pin. Unfold the turning to single width again. Double the other turning and mark where it falls on the other edge fold with a pin. Unfold to single width again and press in the fabric from pin to pin at an angle. Double the turnings and the corner of the hem will fold into a neat mitre. Slipstitch its edges together.

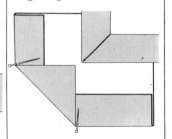

STITCHING A MITRE

This technique is used when the fabric is very bulky or an extra neat finish is required.

Single hem
Follow the instructions for a single hem, previous section, up to pressing in the corner at an angle.

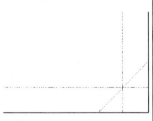

Open out the corner and refold it diagonally with right sides together, raw edges even. Stitch along the diagonal crease from the raw edge to the diagonal fold.

Trim off the corner to within 6mm ($\frac{1}{4}$in) of the stitching and press the seam open.

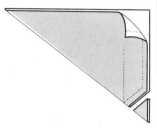

Refold the corner, carefully pushing out the point.

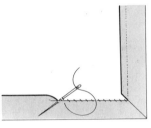

Uneven width hem
Turn under the fabric along both edges for the required amount and press. Turn under the raw edges by 6mm ($\frac{1}{4}$in), press and unfold again. Mark where the turnings intersect and fold in and press the corner (see Single hem, previous section). Refold the corner diagonally as given in the instructions for the above and stitch along the diagonal crease from the 6mm ($\frac{1}{4}$in) crease line. Trim the corner and then turn under the raw edges and machine stitch or hem by hand.

DECORATIVE TRIMMINGS

BUYING DECORATIVE TRIMMINGS

These include braids, ribbons and lace, various cords, fringes and bindings. When buying trimmings, allow an extra length for seams, mitring corners and neatening ends and check that the trimming is colour fast and will not shrink if it is to be applied to a washable object.

APPLYING BRAIDS AND RIBBONS

When stitching braids and ribbons along both edges to fabric, machine topstitch or zigzag in place or sew to the fabric by hand. Alternatively use machine or hand embroidery.

Narrow trimmings should be topstitched to the fabric straight down the centre.

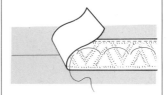

Positioning a trimming

Mark a line along the fabric to indicate where you want the centre of the trimming to fall. Tack the trimming in place, centring it over the marked line.

Some ribbons, especially satin, are marked permanently by a needle, so tack in place close to the edges.

When stitching velvet trimming, use a zipper foot on the machine to avoid crushing the pile.

APPLYING LACE

Lace is usually used for edgings and insertion. The way it is applied to an edge depends on the way the lace has been finished.

If the edge is neatened, topstitch in place over a narrow machine-stitched hem turned to the right side of the fabric.

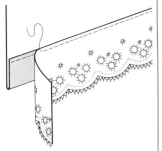

Alternatively, if the edge is unfinished, stitch the lace to the fabric edge, with right sides together, taking a 6mm ($\frac{1}{4}$in) seam allowance. Press the seam upwards and oversew the edges to neaten.

When applying lace insertion, position the lace in the same way as for braids and ribbons and tack in place. Stitch the lace to the fabric close to its edges. Mitre any corners as explained in braids and ribbons. Cut away the fabric from underneath, leaving 6mm ($\frac{1}{4}$in) edges. Turn back the edges and oversew to neaten.

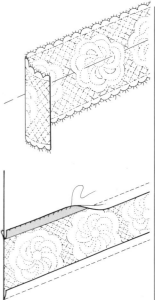

Mitring braids and ribbons

To reduce bulk when turning a corner trimmings should be mitred. The following technique applies to trimmings that are sewn flat on to the fabric along either edge.

Tack the trimming in place along the first side, then topstitch to the fabric along the inner edge, ending at the inner corner. Bring the trimming down to the outer corner and fold back on itself. Stitch the diagonal line between inner and outer corners through all layers. Clip the fold of trimming to 6mm ($\frac{1}{4}$in).

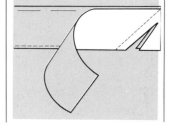

To mitre loose ends of trimming, tack to within 10cm (4in) of the last corner. Press under the end you are working on diagonally in line with the corner. With the right sides of the trimming together, stitch through all layers along the diagonal crease and trim the end.

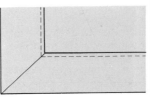

Turn the trimming to the right side and finish stitching in place.

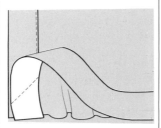

ATTACHING PURCHASED FRINGES

Depending on whether you wish the upper edge of the fringe to show, attach to the inside or outside edge of the fabric. The fringe can be machine stitched in place over a narrow hem. For a more unobtrusive finish, hem the upper and lower edge of the fringe in place by hand.

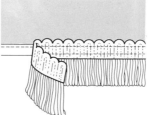

202

APPLYING BINDING

Purchased ribbons or strips of fabric cut on the straight grain can be used to bind straight edges. However, on a curved edge and for a smoother finish on straight edges, bias binding should be used. Either buy ready-made bias binding or make bias strips following the instructions given in PIPING.

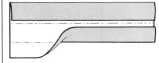

Each strip of home-made bias binding should measure four times the finished width. Press the binding in half lengthways with wrong sides together and then press under the raw edges so they nearly meet at the crease.

The simplest method of applying binding is to fold it over the raw edge and pin and topstitch in place through all thicknesses. Fold the binding diagonally when turning corners to form a neat mitre.

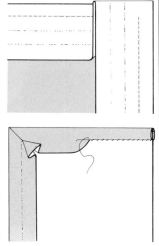

If you do not want a topstitched finish seam the binding to the fabric.

Open out the binding and, right sides together, position the side crease against the fabric seamline. Pin and stitch in place. Turn the binding over the raw edge to the opposite side and hemstitch in place over the line of machine stitching.

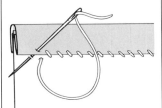

Mitring binding

When seaming binding to an edge the corners should be mitred as follows.

Position the binding against the fabric seamline, right sides together, and stitch along one edge to the seamline corner point.

Raise the presser foot and needle to turn the corner and fold the binding back over the stitched length so that the fold is in line with the stitched edge. Lower the presser foot and stitch the binding to the second edge.

Fold back the binding in this way at every corner and then turn the binding over the raw edges and press the corners into neat mitres on both sides.

APPLYING DECORATIVE CORD TO A STITCHED SEAM

Leave a small centrally placed gap in the seam. Cut the cord about 5cm (2in) longer than the distance needed. Tuck one end inside the seam opening, fastening the thread on the underside and stitch the cord along the seamline by hand, taking small evenly spaced stitches as shown. At the join, tuck

the remaining end inside the seam, overlapping the ends inside. Stitch the length of cord together where it crosses on the outside and then stitch it to the fabric. Try to position the join in an inconspicuous place.

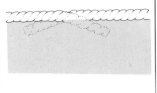

PIPING

Piping is a strip of bias-cut fabric inserted in the seamlines of home furnishings to give a professional finish and a longer life.

There are two types of piping: corded and flat. In corded piping the fabric strip is folded in half around a

length of piping cord. Flat piping consists of the folded fabric strip only. Both types are inserted in the same way.

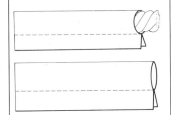

Piping can be bought in thicknesses ranging from 00 to 6. Four, 5 and 6 are the ones most commonly used in home furnishing. Before you buy, check that the cord is pre-shrunk. If not, wash and dry the cord before use.

To estimate the amount of piping cord you need, measure all the seamlines and edges to be finished, adding an extra 5cm (2in) for each join.

Cutting bias strips

Fold the fabric so that the selvedge lies exactly parallel to the crossways grain of the fabric. Press along the fold; the resultant crease marks the bias. Cut off the corner along the crease and then mark the strips in tailor's chalk parallel to this bias edge, using a ruler made in card to the correct strip width. This is calculated by doubling the seam allowance of 1.5cm ($\frac{5}{8}$in) and adding the circumference of the piping cord.

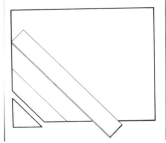

To obtain the length of piping needed, strips usually have to be joined. With right sides together, match the slanted edges as shown. Stitch along the join taking a 6mm (¼in) seam allowance. Press the seam open.

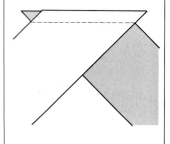

Cutting a continuous bias strip

When extra long lengths of piping are needed, such as for loose covers, this second method can be used.

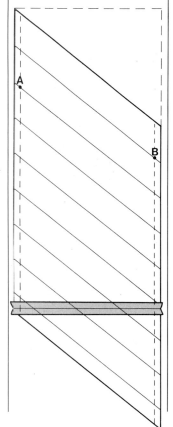

Cut a rectangle of fabric; the length must be at least twice the width. Fold up the bottom left-hand corner so that the crossways edge is aligned with the selvedge. Press. Cut off the corner and stitch to the other edge with right sides facing, taking a 6mm (¼in) seam allowance. Press the seam open.

Rule off the strip widths on the right side of the fabric, parallel to the ends (see previous method).

Then mark a 6mm (¼in) seam allowance along the sides. Mark points A and B on the seamline as shown.

Stick a pin through the wrong side of the fabric at point A and bring it across through point B. Pin the two points together accurately, right sides facing. Next pin the sides together along the marked seamline to form a tubular shape with a seam running diagonally round it.

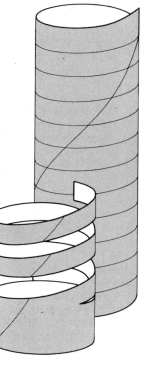

Turn to the right side and check that the ruled lines meet exactly. Turn back to the inside and tack, stitch and press open the seam. With the right side facing, start cutting along the ruled lines in a spiral.

Covering the cord

To cover the piping cord, fold the fabric strip around the cord right side out, raw edges matching. Pin and stitch close to the cord, using a zipper foot on the machine.

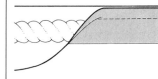

Applying piping to a seam

Lay the piping on the right side of one of the pieces to be seamed, with the stitching matching the fabric seamline, raw edges even. Pin and stitch in place using a zipper foot. If any corners have to be worked round, cut into the piping fabric from the corner point to the stitching.

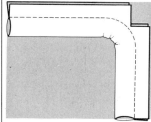

Next, place the other piece of fabric on top of the piped edge, right sides together, edges even. Pin and stitch the seam through all layers, just inside the previous line of stitching.

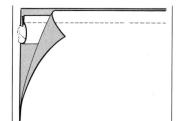

Joining corded piping

If a length of piping goes all the way round an object the ends must be joined. Allow an extra 5cm (2in) for the join.

Begin stitching the covered cord in place 1cm (⅜in) from one end of the piping and stop sewing 5cm (2in) from where you began to stitch. Then unravel the stitches of the piping strip for 2cm (¾in) from the end and fold back the fabric. Trim the cord so that the ends butt.

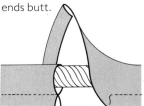

Unfold the fabric so that it overlaps the butted ends. Turn the raw edge under 6mm (¼in) and complete the stitching across the join. Try to position the join either at a seamline or centrally between two edges.

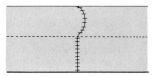

FRILLS AND PLEATS

FRILLS

Edges of home furnishings can be finished with either single or double frills. The fullness of a frill can vary between one and a half to three times the length of the edge to which it is to be attached, depending on the fabric weight and desired effect.

Single frill
Calculate the depth of the frill. Add a 1.5cm ($\frac{5}{8}$in) seam allowance and, depending on the fabric thickness, a double hem allowance of 1cm to 2cm ($\frac{3}{8}$in–$\frac{3}{4}$in).

Join the short edges together with flat fell seams to make a longer or continuous length. If the frill is not continuous, make a double turning of 6mm ($\frac{1}{4}$in) at each end and stitch. Turn up a double hem along the lower edge of the frill and stitch.

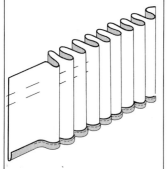

Gather the raw edge to the required size. For long frills, divide the frill and the main fabric edge into an equal number of sections. Work two rows of gathering stitches in each frill section and gather up to fit the corresponding main edge sections. With right sides together, pin the frill to the main fabric edge, tack and stitch in place. Neaten the seam with machine zigzagging and press upwards or make a self-bound seam, trimming down the frill seam to 6mm ($\frac{1}{4}$in).

Double frill
This frill eliminates the need for a hem and produces a full and luxurious look.

Cut double the required depth plus twice the top seam allowance. Join the lengths together with plain seams (double stitched if necessary for strength). Then fold the frill in half, matching raw edges, and gather the top in the same way as for a single frill.

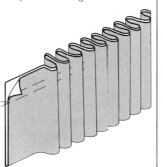

PLEATS

There are three main types of pleat that can be used on home furnishings. For each pleat you will need three times the pleat width (the part visible when the pleat is stitched in place) in fabric.

It is essential that pleats hang correctly, so the pleat strips must be cut with the depth following the straight grain and the long edges of each strip parallel to the crossways grain. When folding pleats work on a flat surface to keep them smooth.

Adjust the width of the pleats so that they break evenly at any corners.

Knife pleats
These pleats lie in the same direction.

Begin by deciding on an appropriate pleat width. Next measure the edge to which the pleats are to be attached and divide this by the pleat width. This gives the number of pleats.

Multiply this number by three to get the width of fabric needed for making up the pleated section and add allowances for seams and side hems, if any.

Decide on the depth of the pleats and add on allowances for the seam and a double or single hem.

Join widths together as necessary, using flat fell seams if the section is to be left unlined and plain seams if a lining is to be attached. Try to position seams in the fold-back section of a pleat. Pin and stitch the hem.

The positioning lines for each pleat should be marked next, at right angles to the fabric edge. Mark the pleat line (A) first, and then measure twice the pleat width from this line and mark the placement line (B). Leave a pleat width gap and return to the beginning of the sequence and repeat until the end of the section is reached.

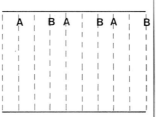

Fold the fabric on the first pleat line and bring to the corresponding placement line. Pin. Repeat until all the fabric has been pleated. Tack along the top and bottom of the pleats and press to hold in place. Stitch in place as required.

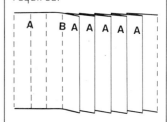

Inverted box pleats
These pleats consist of two pleats folded so that they turn towards each other.

Mark the fabric with a pleat line (A); measure twice the pleat width, then mark a placement line (B). Measure twice the pleat width again and mark the next pleat line. Repeat the sequence from the beginning.

When pleating the fabric, the two pleat lines fold inwards to meet together over the placement line.

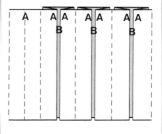

Box pleats
Box pleating is the reverse side of inverted box pleating. Repeat the line sequence of placement line (B), pleat line (A), pleat line (A). Fold the pleat lines *outwards* to meet over the placement lines.

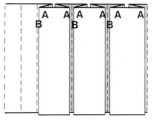

HEADINGS, TRACKS AND POLES

HEADINGS

If a curtain is not to have a valance or pelmet, the heading becomes an important feature. An easy way of producing a decorative effect is to use one of the numerous styles of commercial heading tape.

These narrow strips of strong fabric have slots for the hooks that attach the curtain to the runner on the curtain track. Available in a variety of sizes and weights and a limited range of colours, the tapes usually have two or more drawstrings that pull up to form a gathered or pleated curtain heading. The deeper tapes have more than one row of slots so that the height of the curtain above the track can be adjusted by inserting the hooks in either row of slots.

Choosing tape

Choose the tape that produces the style of heading you want, checking that the tape is suitable for the type of fabric to be used. When calculating the width of fabric needed for the curtains, remember that some tapes gather the fabric more than others.

With pairs of curtains it is important that the design of the heading tape should match across the curtains when they are drawn, unless there is an overlap arm on the track. This is particularly important with triple and cartridge pleats where there is a wide gap between each group of pleats. To achieve even spacing, always begin by placing the heading tape against the curtain edge that will meet in the centre of the window, starting the tape in the middle of a pleat group.

Plain fabrics look good with almost any heading tape, but with patterned fabrics you need to consider how the pleating will affect the design – it could spoil it or produce annoying optical effects.

Sheer fabric can be given body along the heading by using an iron-on stiffener.

Standard gathered tape

This produces a simple gathered heading that is suitable for use on small lightweight curtains or those whose heading will be hidden by a pelmet/valance.

Fabric fullness required: one and a half to two times the track width.

Pencil pleat tape

When tightly pulled up, stiffened pencil pleat tape gives a tailored effect suitable for most types of curtain. However, for lightweight fabrics and sheers, a spaced pencil pleat tape can be bought which produces a softer effect. The tape varies in depth from 4cm to 15cm (1½in–6in).

Fabric fullness required: two and a quarter times the track width.

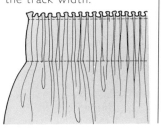

Triple pleat tape (also called pinch pleat)

This tape forms a stiff deep heading suitable for formal lined curtains. The depth varies between 4cm (1½in) and 14cm (5½in). Care must be taken not to crease the space between the pleats when pulling up the cords. Alternatively, use the uncorded type which is pleated manually, by inserting pleater hooks at intervals, to produce single, double, or triple pleats with a crisp, neat finish. Plan where the pleats will come before attaching the heading.

Fabric fullness required: two times the track width.

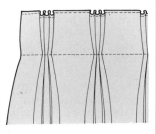

Box pleat tape

This gives a formal appearance which looks good on thicker lined curtains. As it makes the fabric drape into neat folds, it also suits full-length curtains which are hung under a pelmet or valance.

Fabric fullness required: two and a half times the track width.

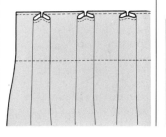

Cartridge pleat tape

When drawn up, this tape produces cylindrical pleats and it is especially suitable for heavy, lined, floor-length curtains. Goblet shaped pleats can be made by pinching in each pleat at the base and securing with a few stitches.

Fabric fullness required: two and a half times the track width.

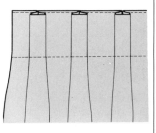

Attaching heading tape

Cut a length of heading tape to the width of the curtain plus 5cm (2in) for end turnings.

Measure from the lower edge of the curtain to obtain the correct position for the tape, taking the measurement to curtain hook height on the track or pole. Mark a line across the curtain.

Measure from the top of the heading tape slots to the edge of the tape. Measure this distance from the marked line and fold over the curtain along this level. Pin the heading tape in position 3mm (⅛in) from the curtain top.

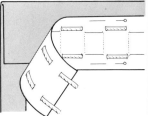

At the inside edge of the curtain pull the cords from the wrong side of the tape for 2.5cm (1in) and knot; turn under the end for 2.5cm (1in). Repeat at the outside edge of the curtain, but pull the cords from the front side of the tape.

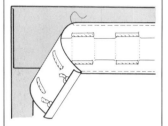

Tack and stitch the tape in place, stitching along the top edge first and taking care not to sew down the knotted cords at the outside curtain edge. Stitch the base edge of the tape in the same direction as the top to prevent puckering.

Draw up the tape and gather the curtain. Wind the surplus cords around a cord tidy or tie in a loose knot. Do not cut.

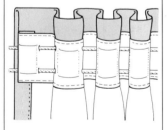

If a frilled heading is required above standard gathered tape, allow for the depth when turning over the curtain top.

TRACKS AND POLES

So many different tracks, rods, poles and fittings are available that it is sometimes difficult to know which to choose. Some manufacturers produce booklets to help with the choice of tracks and accessories and most large department stores have displays of curtain hardware where one can compare differences and functions. The following points should be considered before you buy.
1. Make sure that the track/pole will be strong enough to carry the curtains. Many plastic tracks are not strong enough to bear ones that are heavy or interlined.
2. If buying hardware for net or sheer curtains, choose special inexpensive rods or lightweight tracks. These can be bought for ceiling or wall fixing, with or without a cording set. Some tracks are available with double fittings that enable sheer curtains to be hung on an inner track with the main curtains on the outer one. Tension rods are also available that spring out to grip the inside of the window frame.
3. If the track is going to show, choose one that is fairly unobtrusive, or a decorative one that fits in with the style of curtaining. Some tracks can be covered with fabric or wallpaper.
4. Poles are decorative features in themselves. Decide what type is appropriate for the room and curtain style. Some wooden poles can be covered with fabric or painted or varnished to fit in with a decorating scheme; they can also be

mitred to fit round bay windows. Most poles are packed complete with all the necessary rings, brackets, screws and finials. Some are extendible.
5. Make sure that the track or pole will hold the curtains away from the frame if hanging curtains across a door. Otherwise buy a movable rod that swings the curtain away from the door. For glazed doors special rods can be fixed to the top and bottom so that the curtain hangs close to the glass.
6. Choose a flexible track that will bend easily if you are making curtains to go around a curved window.
7. If curtains are to be constantly handled or are very heavy, get a track or pole with a cording system built in. Cording sets can also be added if the track doesn't have an integral system. Also available are curtain rod pulls that are attached to the lead runner at the centre of the window and hidden behind the edge of the curtain.
8. Weights can be inserted in the hems of lightweight curtains to improve their draping qualities. Leadweight tape can be bought by the metre (yard); alternatively small lead weights can be stitched into the mitre at each curtain corner.
9. If a pelmet or valance is to be used, the track will be purely functional. Remember to choose one that will support the curtains. Some manufacturers offer track and valance rails combined in one fitting.
10. When buying a track

or pole remember to allow for extensions at either side of the window to hold the curtain when it is drawn back and to let in light. The space at each side can vary between 15cm (6in) and 46cm (18in), depending on the window width and the thickness of the curtain fabric.

Positioning the track

Always follow the fixing instructions that come with your chosen track, but as a general guide to fixing tracks follow the instructions below.

Measure the width of the window and cut the track to this length plus an allowance for side extensions (see above).

Lightly pencil a positioning line for the track between 8cm (3in) and 12cm (5in) above the window.

Fix a bracket 2.5cm (1in) in from either end of this marked line. Space the remaining brackets in between at about 30cm (12in) intervals.

Clip the track on to the brackets. Slot the required amount of runners along the tracks (equal to the curtain hooks) and then fix stops at either end.

Curtain poles are fixed to the wall in the same way.

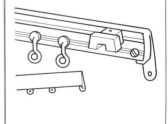

FASTENINGS

The rule for fastenings used on soft furnishings is that the fastening should be appropriate to the weight of fabric and type of furnishing. Zips are best confined to cushion covers and heavy-duty hooks and eyes should be used on loose chair covers.

If you are using press fastener tape, try to match it to the furnishing fabric.

Besides securing wadding in place or fastening an opening, buttons are decorative. Attach small pearly ones to the opening of lace-trimmed pillowcases.

BUTTONS

At the marked position for the button, secure the thread on the right side of the fabric. Slide the button over the needle. Place a matchstick over the top of the button and work stitches over it through the holes of the button.

Remove the matchstick and pull the button up so the slack in the threads is underneath.

Wind the working thread around the slack to make a shank for the button. Fasten off into this shank.

When the button has a shank, secure the thread first, and then take about 12 stitches through the shank and into the fabric then fasten off.

PRESS FASTENERS

Separate the two halves – the ball half should be stitched to the overlapping fabric and the curved socket to the underlap.

Position the top half of the fastener to the fabric at least 6mm ($\frac{1}{4}$in) in from the edge.

Secure the thread underneath and work five or six stitches through each of the holes, taking the needle under the fastener to the next hole. Fasten off the thread.

Position and stitch down the opposite half in the same way.

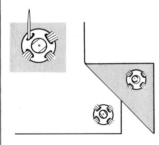

PRESS FASTENER TAPE

This is a length of woven tape with the press fasteners fixed in place at various set intervals. It comes in several widths.

Separate the two layers and, as for single fasteners, stitch the ball half to the top layer and the socket layer to the underneath. Pin and stitch the tape in place down the long edges, using a zipper foot if sewn by machine.

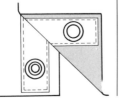

PRESS STUD FASTENERS

There are several types of clamp-on stud on the market and usually they are sold with the special tool for fixing the studs in place. In each case there are two parts to each section that fasten in place on either side of the fabric.

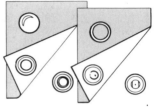

HOOKS AND EYES OR BARS

Stitch the hook to the overlapping layer of fabric and the eye or bar to the underneath.

After securing the thread, hold the hook firmly and work five to six stitches around the first loop, then take the needle through the fabric to the second loop and repeat. Take the needle through the fabric to the head of the hook and work several stitches around the hook. Fasten off.

Stitch through the loops of the eyes or bar in the same way.

TOUCH AND CLOSE FASTENING

This fastener consists of two strips of material, one covered in loops and the other with small hooks, which cling together when pressed. It is available in various widths and colours. Choose the right weight for the job and stitch in place in the same way as tape.

TOUCH AND CLOSE SPOTS

The same type of material as before, but it comes in small discs. Hold in place with a triangle of stitching across the disc.

ZIP FASTENERS

Zips come in varying weights with nylon or metal teeth. Nylon zips are available in a wider range of colours and are more flexible, but take care when ironing as a hot iron may damage the teeth. Use a heavy-duty zip when a closing will be subjected to a lot of strain.

Inserting a centred open-end zip

Stitch the seam up to the zip opening and then reverse to secure the stitching. Machine tack the zip opening. Press the seam open.

Place the zip face downwards over the seam allowances with the bottom stop 3mm ($\frac{1}{8}$in) below the beginning of the tacked section with the teeth centred exactly over the seamline.

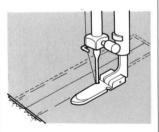

Pin and tack in place through all layers on either side of the zip, 6mm ($\frac{1}{4}$in) from the teeth. Turn to the right side. Topstitch the zip in place just inside the tacking lines using a zipper foot on the machine and pivoting at the bottom end corners. Pull the threads to the opposite side and tie securely. Remove the tacking from the zip opening.

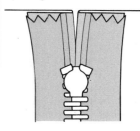

If you wish to prevent the stitches widening at the slider, unpick 8cm (3in) of the tacking and ease the slider down past the foot. Complete the machining.

Inserting an enclosed centred zip

If the zip is to be placed in an enclosed seam the zip opening should measure 1cm ($\frac{3}{8}$in) longer than the zip teeth (including the top and bottom stop). Whipstitch the zip tapes together above the top stop before beginning zip application.

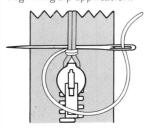

Where possible, apply the zip to flat fabric.

The seam is stitched in the same way as for an open-end zip, but at the top of the tacked opening backstitch two stitches and then resume stitching at the normal length. Press the seam open.

Sew across both ends when tacking and topstitching in place.

Inserting a zip in a piped seam

Pipe one edge of the seam but do not close the opening.

Open the zip and place it face down on the piped seam with the teeth in line with the piping stitching. Tack the zip in place, then stitch along the seam 3mm ($\frac{1}{8}$in) from the teeth.

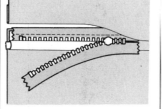

Turn back the seam allowance so that the piping lies at the edge of the opening. Close the zip. Press under the seam allowance of the other piece of fabric. Bring the folded edge over the zip so that it meets the piping. Tack the length of the seam through all thicknesses and then machine stitch 6mm ($\frac{1}{4}$in) from the folded edge and across the end(s) of the zip up to the piping. Take the threads through to the wrong side of the work and tie them. Press.

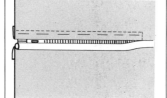

Applying a zip to delicate fabrics

On delicate fabrics and on those with a nap, such as velvet, the final topstitching can be worked by hand using prickstitch, a very small backstitch.

KNOTS

Slip knot

Hold the two twine ends in one hand. Put the right end over the left and bring it back round over the left end again. Pull the right end up through the loop that has been formed. Pull to tighten.

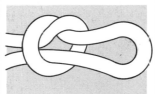

Reef knot

Place the right twine end over left and tie a knot. Bring the left twine end over the right and knot again. Pull to tighten.

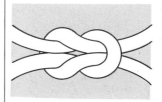

ROULEAU

This refers to a narrow tube of fabric made from bias strips.

Cut enough bias strips 2.5cm to 3cm (1in–1$\frac{1}{4}$in) wide to obtain the desired length of the rouleau, and stitch them together (see PIPING). With right sides together, fold the strip in half lengthways and stitch 6mm ($\frac{1}{4}$in) from the edge. Do not trim the seam allowances as these help pad the rouleau. Sew the end of the tube on to the eye of a blunt-ended tapestry needle and push

this through the tube to turn it the right side out. Detach the tube from the needle.

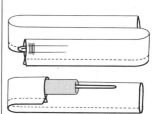

Making loop buttonholes

Make a rouleau to the required length as described above. Place the end of the rouleau to the edge of the item on the right side. Pin in position, making the loops the size required to fit the button, and leaving approximately 6mm ($\frac{1}{4}$in) between the loops if any space is desired. Tack and stitch the loops in place before attaching the facing.

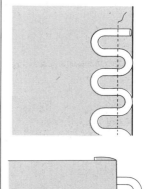

CARE, CLEANING AND REPAIR

GENERAL CARE

Keep upholstery and soft furnishings looking good with regular cleaning and, if necessary, with effective yet discreet repairs.

Vacuum upholstery regularly to remove day-to-day dust and fluff. Do not brush the fabric as this simply shifts the dust from one spot to another. Plump up loose cushions daily and if they are not shaped turn once a week. Use a barely damp sponge or a length of sticky tape to remove cat and dog hairs.

Keep delicate fabrics out of direct sunlight and away from strong heat sources. If sunlight is strong, draw the curtains or blinds. Position chairs and sofas away from open fires and radiators.

If a cotton or linen fabric loses its crispness after washing, use spray starch just before ironing to add extra body to the fabric. Do not use starch if the fabric is glazed or crease-resistant.

CLEANING

Cleaning curtains

When buying fabric for making curtains always look for instructions on how to care for it, usually given on a label or printed on the selvedge. Most manufacturers use the International Care Labelling Code symbols, which tell you the maximum wash, if the fabric should be spun, how to rinse, dry and iron it and whether it should be dry cleaned.

To wash heading-taped curtains, remove the hooks from the tape and let out the gathers (do not cut the gathering string). Shake the curtains to remove any dust then soak them for about 10 minutes in cold water with a little liquid detergent. Rinse, then wash at the appropriate machine setting.

Wash net curtains frequently to keep them fresh and clean. Soak first in cold water and detergent as before, then machine or hand wash in hand-hot water (as hot as the hand can bear). Do not wring but give them a short machine spin. Tumble dry on the lowest setting to prevent creasing, or dry iron on a warm setting then hang immediately.

If necessary use a brand-name whitener to brighten dull net curtains.

Curtains that are interlined or have milium insulated lining should be dry cleaned.

Cleaning upholstery

Fixed upholstery can be shampooed *in situ* to remove general grubbiness. Use a brand-name upholstery shampoo, following the maker's instructions. Always test the products first on an inconspicuous piece of the upholstery to see how the fabric reacts.

Vacuum the upholstery before and after shampooing and be careful not to saturate the fabric as the padding and backing underneath may shrink.

Washing lampshades

Remove the shade from the lamp and take off any coloured trimming that may run when wet. Dip the whole shade into a bowl of warm soapy water and then rinse with clean water. Dry the shade away from direct heat.

Non-washable fabric shades are best cleaned by a professional, but dust regularly and remove any greasy marks with a brand-name stain removal solvent.

CLEANING LOOSE COVERS

If you have no precise care information and you are not sure what the covers are made of, it is advisable to get them dry cleaned. Always test for colour fastness before washing coloured covers and wash them separately if they are not fast or have them dry cleaned. Dry cleaning is advisable for multicoloured covers.

Cotton and linen fabrics will shrink in the wash – usually to 95 per cent of their original size. If your covers are not loose enough to take this, then they should be dry cleaned. Washing can cause piping to shrink and pucker unless the cord was shrunk before being covered.

1) Vacuum the covers thoroughly, using the vacuum-cleaner attachment, while the covers are still in place. Remove any pet hairs.

2) Next remove the covers. Check for any tear or holes and mend as necessary before washing. Fasten any cushion zips otherwise they may get broken.

3) Wash by hand or machine, selecting the suitable programme for the fabric. Hang the covers until they are almost dry.

4) Iron them while they are still slightly damp – on the wrong side if the fabric has a matt finish and on the right side if it is shiny.

5) Put the covers back on and finish ironing the seat and back – place a cloth over the fabric and iron through it if the cover fabric has a matt finish.

6) If you find that the covers have shrunk during washing and you cannot fit them back on the chair or sofa, re-wet them and then carefully stretch back on while very damp.

7) Having made sure that the lines of piping are all in correct position, iron the covers until they are dry.

REMOVING STAINS

If possible remedial action should be taken as soon as a stain occurs. This will limit the damage to the fabric or make further stain removal treatment unnecessary.

Non greasy stains can be rinsed or sponged with cold water and salt thrown on to red wine, fruit and beetroot stains to stop them from spreading. Oily stains can be sprinkled with talcum powder to absorb the grease.

Leave washable items to soak in cold water if you cannot work on them immediately. However, never soak wool, silk or fabric with a flame-resistant finish.

Apart from these immediate first aid measures, always test any removal treatment on an inconspicuous area of fabric before tackling the real thing. Water can make marks on delicate fabrics; some solvents can strip dye.

Repeat mild stain removal treatments rather than go for an all-out attack with a heavy-duty solvent, otherwise the fabric might be damaged.

Treatment should be confined to a circular area around the stain, working from the outside to the middle. This prevents the stain spreading and the treatment leaving a dirty ring.

Try to lift stains off fabric rather than push them further in: dab at them rather than rub. Treat a surface stain from the underside of the fabric, holding a dry absorbent pad over the stain to stop it being re-deposited on the surface as you work on it from the back.

Always use a pad of *white* absorbent cloth, like a piece of muslin or cotton to dab on alcohol- or water-based solvents. The dye in coloured cloth can be affected by certain chemicals.

Professional cleaning is advisable for any difficult or unidentified stain. Some dry cleaners will treat fixed upholstery in your home. Don't overwet this type of upholstery when tackling a stain yourself.

SAFETY PRECAUTIONS

Remember that the majority of solvents and bleaches used in stain removal are either poisonous, flammable or dangerous to inhale; many are a combination of all three. Therefore simple safety precautions should be observed.

Keep all stain removal products away from children, preferably in a locked cupboard. Products should always be carefully labelled and never poured into soft drinks bottles.

Work in a well-ventilated area with a window or door open. Wear rubber gloves to protect your skin. Never smoke while handling solvents or use them in a room where there is an open fire or a heater burning. Turn off any pilot lights.

STAIN REMOVAL AGENTS

The following list gives details of some of the most useful stain removal agents and how to use them.

Ammonia will neutralize acid marks. Dilute 1 part ammonia to 3 parts water. Avoid contact with skin, eyes and clothing. Ammonia can make certain dyes run so test on an inconspicuous patch before tackling a stain on coloured fabric. Do not use on wool.

Enzyme (biological) detergent removes protein stains such as blood, gravy, milk and egg. Follow the manufacturer's instructions on the length of soak and wash. It should not be used on wool, silk, non-fast coloureds, flame-resistant or rubberized fabrics. Don't soak any item with metal fastenings.

Glycerine softens stains thus making them easier to remove. It can be used on any fabric and any colour. Dilute 1 part glycerine with 1 part warm water. Work into the fabric and leave for an hour. Remove by sponging with warm water.

Household borax is a mild alkali that works on acid stains. Soak washable fabrics for 10 to 15 minutes in a solution of 1 tablespoon of borax to 600ml (1 pint) of warm water. Soaking coloured fabrics for any longer could result in slight bleaching.

Hydrogen peroxide is a mild slow-acting bleach. Use 20 volume strength and dilute 1 part hydrogen peroxide to 6 parts water. Do not use it on nylon or flame-resistant fabrics. Most fabrics can be soaked in hydrogen peroxide for up to 30 minutes, but it will have a slight bleaching effect on coloured fabrics. To speed the stain removing on coloureds you can therefore add half a teaspoon of ammonia to each litre (1¾ pints) of hydrogen peroxide and water solution.

Methylated spirit (metholated alcohol) should be used neat, dabbed on to the stain. Test it on an inconspicuous area when treating coloured fabric as it can make some dyes run. Buy the white rather than the violet variety as the violet colour can mark some delicate fabrics. It is highly flammable and poisonous. Don't use on triacetates and acetates.

Stain-removing kits can be bought that deal with most household stains on a variety of surfaces, including upholstery. They consist of small containers of chemicals that you can use separately or mixed together according to the type of stain.

Solvents will dissolve grease, oil marks and other kinds of stains. Brand-name solvents or stain removers come in liquid, paste and aerosol form. Follow the maker's instructions exactly.

Other useful generic solvents are amyl acetate, white spirit (white alcohol), and non-oily nail polish remover (don't use this on acetate or triacetate fabrics). The majority of solvents are flammable.

STAIN REMOVAL

Always refer to the treatment list before using any of the solvents and bleaches mentioned

STAIN	WASHABLE FABRICS	NON-WASHABLE FABRICS & FIXED UPHOLSTERY
ADHESIVES Any type of adhesive is difficult to remove when set. Old stains should always be tackled by professional cleaners. Do not try to remove adhesive from pile fabrics.	**Clear household glue:** dab lightly with non oily nail varnish remover, working from the back of the stain, and holding a pad over the mark on the other side. Use amyl acetate on triacetate and acetate. **Contact adhesives:** as above. **Epoxy Resin:** as above. On synthetic fabrics use lighter fuel. Dried stains will be impossible to remove. **Superglue:** act *immediately*. Saturate the cleaning pad with water and hold on the affected area until the glue loosens.	As for washable fabrics. Do not use lighter fuel on upholstery. Follow any treatment with upholstery shampoo.
BLOOD	Sponge fresh bloodstains with cold salt water, then soak in an enzyme detergent solution if the fabric is suitable. Dried stains and those that cannot be soaked in enzyme detergent may need a soaking in a hydrogen peroxide solution. A dilute solution of household bleach can be used on white cottons and linens. See the manufacturer's instructions.	Sponge with cold water to which you have added a few drops of ammonia. Rinse with clear water and blot well.
CANDLEWAX Do not pick wax off pile fabric unless it comes away easily. When de-waxing pile fabrics apply blotting paper to the front and iron from the back. Gently brush up the pile with a fine toothbrush after treatment.	Pick off excess wax with a blunt knife, then sandwich the stain between two sheets of blotting or brown paper and run a warm iron over the top to melt it. Use a grease solvent to remove any remaining stain and wash as normal to remove any colour left by a coloured candle.	Non-washable fabrics can be treated in the same way as washable, using methylated spirit (metholated alcohol) to take out any remaining colour. Use one sheet of paper and the heel of the iron on upholstery. Do not squash pile upholstery. Hold the iron over the blotting paper without pressing down.
CHEWING GUM	Freeze the gum by holding a plastic bag of ice cubes over it until it hardens. It can then be broken up and picked off. Alternatively use a brand-name aerosol gum remover which works in the same way. Any remaining deposit can be removed by a brand-name liquid stain remover.	Use a brand-name chewing gum remover and treat any remaining deposit with a stain remover.

STAIN	WASHABLE FABRICS	NON-WASHABLE FABRICS & FIXED UPHOLSTERY
CHOCOLATE	Scrape off any deposit with a blunt knife. Dab the stain with a glycerine solution. Leave for 10 minutes and then wash at the recommended temperature for the fabric, using an enzyme detergent if possible. If the mark remains use a brand-name stain remover.	Scrape off as much as possible and then use a stain remover. Shampoo upholstery.
COFFEE	Mop up spilled liquid with tissues or paper towels and then soak in a warm enzyme detergent solution. If the fabric is not suitable, soak in a borax solution and then wash at 50°C (120°F). Use a brand-name stain remover to remove any residue when dry. White cottons and linens can be carefully bleached in a hydrogen peroxide solution.	Mop up the spilled liquid. Sponge with a borax solution and then with clear water. Blot dry. Use a stain remover on any residue. Coffee stains on acrylic velvet should be blotted with tissues. Spray the stain with a warm solution of enzyme washing powder, 1 tablespoon to 600ml (1 pint) water, and then rub lightly in the direction of the pile. Old stains should be dabbed with a glycerine solution, left for an hour and then rinsed with a cloth wrung out in warm water. Blot well.
CURRY It is turmeric in curry that leaves the bright yellow stain. As it is a vegetable dye, it can be difficult to remove.	Scrape up any deposit with a spoon or a blunt knife. Tackle fresh stains with a mild borax solution, placing the stained area over a basin and pouring the solution through repeatedly. Work a glycerine solution into stubborn stains, leave for an hour and rinse. Wash in enzyme detergent if suitable for the fabric. Any remaining marks can be bleached out of white fabric with a hydrogen peroxide solution.	Scrape up any deposits. Sponge with a warm borax solution, rinse and blot well. If the stain is not removed, have the item cleaned professionally.
FAT/GREASE/GRAVY	Scrape off any fat or deposits with a blunt knife, then blot the fabric with tissues. A high temperature wash should dissolve grease marks on cotton and linen. Treat stains on delicate fabrics with eucalyptus oil, then wash or sponge. Other fabrics should be treated with a solvent. **Gravy:** soak in cool water and then wash in warm detergent suds. Treat any remaining grease marks when dry.	Scrape off any deposits. Treat with an appropriate grease solvent. Alternatively, spread talcum powder over the mark and brush off when it becomes impregnated with oil. Continue reapplying and brushing off powder until all the grease has been absorbed.

STAIN	WASHABLE FABRICS	NON-WASHABLE FABRICS & FIXED UPHOLSTERY
FRUIT JUICE	Rinse the affected area under the cold tap. Then wash with an enzyme detergent if the fabric is suitable. Dried stains should be lubricated with a glycerine solution and then left for an hour before washing. A brand-name stain remover may deal with obstinate stains, or try soaking fabric in a solution of hydrogen peroxide. Household bleach can be used on white linen and cotton. See the maker's instructions.	Sponge marks with cold water. If stains are not removed, lubricate with a glycerine solution and leave for an hour before sponging with a borax solution. Blot and rinse well. For upholstery, shampoo the affected area after treating with a glycerine solution.
INK The wrong type of treatment may set stains irredeemably, so always identify the type of ink first. Only tackle small fresh stains. All others should be dealt with by a professional cleaner.	**Ballpoint:** dab the stain lightly with methylated spirit (metholated alcohol) or a brand-name ballpoint ink remover. Wash as normal. **Felt tip:** hold water-soluble stains under cold running water until most of the colour is gone and then wash as usual. Blot other stains with methylated spirit (metholated alcohol) or a brand-name removal product. Treat residues with liquid detergent, working well into the fabric. Wash.	Treat stains made by ballpoint and non- water-soluble felt tips with methylated spirit (metholated alcohol) or a brand-name stain remover. For water-soluble ink, sponge with cold water until no more ink can be removed. Allow to dry and treat any remaining mark with a stain remover.
LIPSTICK	Scrape off any surplus with a blunt knife. Dab with a glycerine solution or eucalyptus oil. Leave for an hour, rinse and wash. Bleach out any remaining marks on white fabric using a hydrogen peroxide solution.	Scrape off surplus lipstick and dab the stain with eucalyptus oil or a liquid grease solvent. Shampoo upholstery.
PAINT Never try to remove paint from pile fabrics.	**Emulsion:** scrape off excess wet paint and sponge the stain with cold water. Wash in warm water. Soften dried emulsion stains with methylated spirit (metholated alcohol) or use a brand-name paint removing product formulated for fabric. **Oil-based paint:** scrape off any excess paint and dab stains with white spirit (white alcohol) or a brand-name paint removing product. Sponge with cold water and repeat the treatment if necessary.	Scrape off any excess wet paint and sponge with cold water. Soften dried emulsion stains in the same way as for washables. Professional treatment is needed for dried stains on upholstery and delicate fabrics.

STAIN	WASHABLE FABRICS	NON-WASHABLE FABRICS & FIXED UPHOLSTERY
RUST	Rub the stain with lemon juice and rinse. Do not let the lemon juice dry on the fabric. Alternatively, use a brand-name rust remover, following the manufacturer's instructions.	Use a brand-name rust remover, following the manufacturer's instructions.
SCORCH MARKS Man-made fibres will harden after scorching and the damage is usually irrevocable. Small areas of very badly scorched fabric such as cigarette burns can be cut out and rewoven or invisibly mended.	Slight scorch marks on fabrics made from natural fibres may be removed by brushing with a stiff clothes brush to lift the burnt ends. Otherwise soak in a warm borax solution until the marks have faded. Rinse and wash as usual. Heavy scorching cannot usually be completely removed, although cotton and linen can be bleached in a hydrogen peroxide solution if the fibres are not too badly damaged.	Dab the marks with a glycerine solution and leave for an hour. Then sponge with warm water. For heavier scorches, sponge with a borax solution. Do not overwet. Repeat the treatment if necessary.
URINE Dried stains on non washable fabrics and upholstery require professional cleaning. Do not use white vinegar on acetate or triacetate.	Rinse fresh stains under cold running water and then wash as usual. Dried stains should be soaked in an enzyme detergent solution if the fabric is suitable and then washed in the normal way. Badly stained white cotton and linen can be soaked in a solution of household bleach, following the manufacturer's instructions. Marks on light fabrics can sometimes be reduced by mild bleaching in a hydrogen peroxide solution.	Sponge fresh stains with cold water and blot well. Then sponge with a weak solution of white vinegar and warm water. For upholstery, sponge with an upholstery shampoo to which a few drops of disinfectant have been added.
WINE	Immediately mop up spilled red wine with tissues or kitchen paper and rinse the affected article under tepid running water. Soak any remaining marks in an enzyme detergent solution if the fabric is suitable or sponge with a borax solution. Household bleach can be used to remove stubborn marks on white cotton or linen, following the manufacturer's instructions.	Mop up as much wine as possible and then sponge with warm water. Sprinkle the area with talcum powder while still damp and brush off after 5 minutes. Repeat until the stain has been absorbed. Dried stains should be softened with a glycerine solution and then sponged with a cloth wrung out in warm water and detergent. Then sponge with clear water. Shampoo upholstery after treating with glycerine.

SEWING REPAIRS

Deal with any slits, snags and holes as soon as they occur, before the damage gets any worse.

Patching a hole

If you need to mend a large hole use a piece of the same fabric so the repair will be almost invisible.

With a small pair of scissors, trim the ragged edges of the hole to a square or a rectangle, making sure you cut away all the damaged area. Make a 6mm (¼in) diagonal snip at each corner.

From the repair fabric, cut another square half as large again as the damaged section (if the fabric is patterned, be sure to line up the design accurately).

Lay the patch evenly over the hole, with the right side of the patch to the wrong side of the fabric. Hold the patch in place with tacking. Then turn under the edges of the patch by 1cm (⅜in) and stitch in place.

With the right side of the fabric facing, turn under the edges of the hole all round the patch and stitch in place.

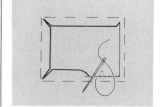

If the fabric is to come under a lot of strain use machine stitching, but on delicate items or where the patch will show slip hem the edges in place.

Mending a tear

If the tear is small and the fabric does not come under much strain, simply oversew the edges together.

Use a length of thread from another section of the fabric if possible – take a length from inside a hem or from a remnant – and catch in both edges of the tear with small stitches.

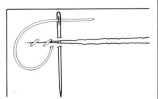

For extra strength, cut a piece of soft iron-on interfacing 1cm (⅜in) larger than the tear. Place it on the wrong side of the fabric over the tear and fix in place using a hot iron; catch the edges in place as before, or machine zigzag them together, working centrally down the tear.

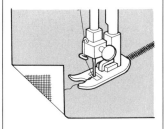

Darning

If the fabric is worn through, the easiest way to strengthen the area is with darning.

Use sewing thread or take some threads from inside the hem or from a remnant. Use a special darning needle, which is long and fine.

Start about 1cm (⅜in) below the worn area and the same distance to one side of it. Follow the line of the original threads and work a row of tiny running stitches across the fabric, finishing 1cm (⅜in) to one side of the worn area; now turn the fabric around and work a second row just above the first one.

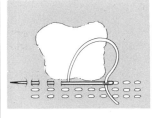

Repeat, continuing over the worn area. Carry the thread across any holes, being careful not to pull too tight.

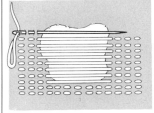

Now turn the work around and work in the opposite direction exactly as before. Weave the needle under and over the first set of threads to create new fabric.

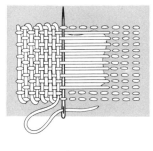

Replacing a decorative button

When replacing a button on a button-backed chair or a cushion, you will need an upholsterer's needle (a special double-pointed needle about 15–20cm/6–8in long), a 30cm (12in) length of twine and an appropriately sized button mold if the original button has been lost.

Cover the button according to the maker's instructions. Look for spare fabric underneath the piece of furniture if you are working on a chair.

Next thread the needle. Holding the unthreaded end of twine, pull the needle through the upholstery until you can see the eye. Do not pull it out completely, but push back through so it comes out about 6mm (¼in) from the entry point.

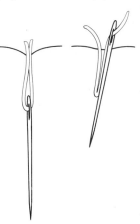

Adjust the twine so that the ends are even and thread one end through the button shank. Holding the pieces of twine together, tie a slip knot (see KNOTS). Tighten the loop, then tie the twine in an ordinary knot finished by a reef knot. Trim the twine, tucking the ends under the button to hide them.

KNOTS   209

PATTERNED FABRICS

MATCHING AND CENTRING PATTERNS

When using a fabric with a distinct woven or printed design, it is often necessary to match the design across seams. This is done by adjusting the fabric pieces against each other lengthways during cutting out so that design repeats are aligned. Fabric is usually printed or woven so that half widths and widths can be attached without adjusting the design to match widthways.

Large designs should match horizontally across adjacent curtains and be positioned in the centre of chair cover sections and cushions.

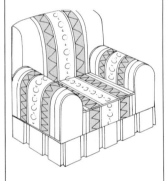

Measuring up patterned fabric

To allow for pattern adjustment, extra fabric has to be added to the basic length required for making a particular item of soft furnishing.

When matching large designs horizontally across adjacent curtains or joining patterned fabric widths to make fuller curtains, measure the height of the design repeat (the distance between the beginning of the design motif and the beginning of the next) and add that measurement to the length of each fabric piece.

Without laying out chair pattern pieces on the fabric it is difficult to calculate how much extra fabric you will need for centring large designs. However, most shop assistants at furnishing fabric counters are well practised in estimating the approximate amount if you give them the dimensions of the furniture to be covered.

Cutting out

For curtains, mark a straight line across the fabric where a row of design repeats begins; this will form the hem foldline. Measure the correct length of the curtain up from this line; add the hem allowance below it. Cut across the fabric at the top and bottom of the curtain.

To cut subsequent lengths, place the cut length and uncut fabric side by side, right sides facing. Adjust the uncut fabric so that the design motifs match across the two pieces of fabric. Cut off the next length, trimming any excess fabric at the base if necessary. Repeat until all the curtain lengths have been cut out.

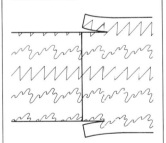

For sofas and chairs, lay the pattern pieces out on the straight grain of the fabric, and juggle the outside back, inside back, outside arm, arm fronts, seat and front

seat and any ungathered skirt pieces until they are each centred over a design motif. If there are any joins across the inside back, seat and seat front of a sofa, allow for the matching of repeats as before.

Joining seams

To match up design motifs across a join the seams have to be tacked together from the right side of the fabric pieces using ladder stitch. If the fabric has been badly printed or has a woven design that tends to repeat unevenly, you may have to ease the seams lengthways so that the design repeats in unbroken sequence across the join.

First turn under the seam allowance along one edge and place over the other unfolded edge so that the pattern matches exactly. Pin in place. Trim down any excess fabric to the seam allowance if necessary. Then ladder stitch across the join. Fold the fabric with right sides together and machine stitch the seams.

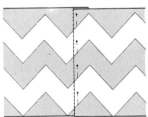

PREPARING TO SEW

Before cutting out, fabric ends should be straightened and the fabric pre-shrunk if need be. It is also helpful to understand the basic facts about fabric structure and the meaning

behind the terminology.

The lengthways grain refers to the warp threads which run the length of the fabric. These are interwoven at right angles by the weft threads, which form the crossways grain. Any diagonal that intersects these two grainlines is a bias. The selvedge is the firmly woven strip formed along the lengthways edges of the finished fabric.

The grains of the fabric have different properties: the lengthways one has very little stretch, the crossways gives more, and the bias stretches the most.

Pre-shrinking

This is advisable if you do not know whether or by how much a washable fabric will shrink. To pre-shrink, wash and dry the fabric following the fabric care instructions often printed on the selvedge.

Straightening the fabric ends

Tearing is suitable for firmly woven fabrics. First snip into one selvedge, grasp the fabric firmly, and rip across to the opposite selvedge. If the strip rips away to nothing part of the way across, repeat, beginning further from the raw edge.

Drawing a thread is more suitable for loosely woven or soft fabrics. Snip into the selvedge, grasp one or two crosswise threads and pull gently. Alternately push the fabric and pull the threads until you reach the opposite selvedge. Cut along the pulled thread.

FABRIC PAINTS

PAINT CHOICE

Fabric paints make it possible to create highly individual printed and painted effects on furnishing fabric without complicated equipment or in-depth knowledge of specialist techniques.

Choose the type of paint that is appropriate for use on the fabric you wish to decorate. Some are suitable for lightweight, light-coloured fabrics, others for darker tones and heavier weights, in wools, silks, synthetics and so on. Felt tip marking pens, designed for painting and drawing on cotton, synthetic and silk fabrics, are also available.

BASIC GUIDELINES

1. Always read the manufacturer's instructions before beginning a project.
2. For the most successful first attempts, stick to closely woven, natural fibres in plain colours.
3. Start in a small way to build up your confidence. Try painting an inexpensive cushion cover before it is made up, experimenting on any spare material before tackling the real thing.
4. Pick the right time and place for fabric painting. You'll need plenty of space and somewhere you can work uninterrupted. Wait for a warm still day if fabric is to be painted and dried outdoors.
5. Protect your working surface with old dust sheets, a layer of polythene sheeting and a top layer of absorbent kitchen paper. Cover yourself in old clothes or an overall. Rubber gloves will be necessary if a painting technique is very messy.

6. Fabrics to be painted should always be newly washed, dry and well pressed. In particular, wash new fabric to remove the manufacturer's finish.
7. So that fabric is held taut while you are painting, pin it over a frame – an empty drawer or old window frame will do – otherwise fix it to a piece of softboard with drawing pins. Large pieces of fabric can be clamped to a table covered in dust sheets and polythene sheeting.
8. The final result of your painting will be affected by the original colour of the fabric. If in doubt how fabric colours and paint will mix, test a small sample piece first.
9. If you do make a mistake while applying paint, immediately rub the affected area vigorously with soap and water, then machine wash or dry clean.
10. When fabric painting has been completed, the colours should be allowed to dry and then fixed permanently. Check what method the fabric paint manufacturer recommends. Many paints are fixed by dry heat, although others are fixed by steaming or being immersed in a water-based fixative solution.

FIRST PROJECT

One of the easiest projects to tackle is painting plain stiffened fabric blinds with bands of colour.

Mark the area to be painted lightly in soft pencil, then apply masking tape along the drawn line, pressing down firmly so fabric paint cannot seep underneath.

Apply undiluted fabric

colour evenly and sparingly with a sponge or fine paintbrush, depending on the thickness of the stripes.

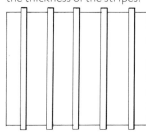

Allow to dry thoroughly before adding a second coat of colour or removing the masking tape.

PAINT EFFECTS

Sponging

This newly revived technique for painting walls can be applied to fabric in the same way, with several complementary shades building up into a marbly effect. This is most striking when used over a large area of fabric, such as curtains.

Dampen the fabric first and pin to the frame (see BASIC GUIDELINES).

Pour small amounts of undiluted fabric paint into dishes and use a separate piece of moist natural sponge to apply each colour. Don't saturate the sponge; only a little paint should be absorbed each time you take up colour.

Experiment on a spare scrap of fabric first and dilute with water if a more subtle,

muted look is required.

Using light even pressure, dab the sponge on to the fabric either across or down from the top, depending on the desired effect. Without waiting for the paint to dry, sponge the next colour directly on top, or in adjacent lines for mottled stripes.

Spray painting

An abundance of unusual textured effects can be achieved using an ordinary household plant spray and a dilute solution of fabric paint.

Spray paint through garden net for a checked pattern, plastic doilies for a lacy texture, or stencils for more uniform designs, and so on.

Be prepared to work outside, either with fabric pegged to a washing line or pinned to a piece of softboard propped up against a wall.

Fix the chosen template in place with pins or paper clips and pour fabric paint into the spray container with roughly half as much water again (check individual manufacturer's instructions for spray painting). Hold the spray 46cm (18in) away from the fabric surface and depress the lever with short, sharp movements.

Work from the top of the fabric downwards, covering one complete area lightly with paint before moving on to the next. Don't overspray, as this will cause unsightly dripping. Leave to dry.

Paint splattering

For a unique 'abstract expressionist' finish, furnishing fabric can be dribbled, flicked and splashed with paint in the same way Jackson Pollock created his pictures. This is a very messy business, so prepare the fabric as for spray-painting and cover yourself up well.

Pour undiluted fabric paints into wide-necked jam jars, colour mixing at this stage if you wish.

Plunge a soft paintbrush into one of the jars and flick the excess paint on to the fabric – don't worry about it

running as this helps give the desired effect. You can also paint in the odd spot, splodge or squiggle to fill in the gaps.

Allow ample drying time for any technique that uses paint as generously as this.

For a finer splattered effect, use an old toothbrush and flick paint on to the fabric by drawing a piece of card across the bristles towards you. Soft flexible bristles and hard stiff bristles give different effects.

STENCILLING

Stencils can be bought in numerous designs from large stationers and craft shops, or you can cut your own from waxed card or stiff plastic.

Centring a stencil

To position a motif accurately when stencilling the middle of a piece of fabric – a tablecloth for example – find the centre of the fabric by folding it in quarters and mark with a pin. Then mark the half folds with two straight lines of pins crossing the central point. These should be slightly longer and wider than the stencil block.

With a pencil rule vertically and horizontally across the stencil. The lines should cross at the centre of the motif. Align them with the corresponding lines of pins and mark the corners of the stencil on the fabric with masking tape. Remove the pins.

To position for stencilling, line up the corners of the stencil with those of the fabric.

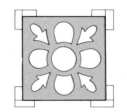

Positioning a stencil across a corner

To centre an irregularly shaped motif across a corner, place the stencil approximately in the desired position. The top of the stencil block should form a diagonal across the corner of the fabric. Mark where this line intersects one of the side edges with a pin.

Measure from the pin to the corner and then mark off this measurement on the other side edge. Press in the corner from pin to pin. Mark the midpoint of this crease.

To paint the motif, align the top of the stencil block against the crease and match

the vertical line on the stencil (see previous method) to the midpoint.

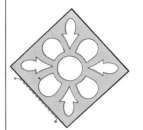

Stencilling a straight border

To repeat a border motif along a straight edged piece of fabric, position the stencil and measure the gap between the bottom of the stencil block and the fabric edge. Keeping this measurement even, mark a horizontal guideline along the fabric.

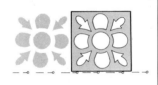

Calculate the repeat length (the length of the motif plus any intervening space before the motif begins again) and the number you wish to fit into the border. If the border turns a corner, motifs should be carefully spaced to take this into account.

Keeping spacing even, move the stencil along the horizontal guideline and, using the sides of the block as a rule, mark the repeat guidelines with a pencil or pins.

Stencilling a circular border

If you are stencilling a circular piece of fabric, mark the border guideline (see previous method) with an improvised compass of string and a pencil or tailor's chalk.

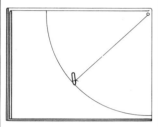

Motif spacing is particularly important when stencilling a circle. Calculate the circumference by multiplying 3.14 by the diameter.

Stencilling an all-over pattern

To stencil a regularly spaced, all-over pattern, a grid must be marked on the fabric.

Draw the dimensions of the fabric to scale on graph paper. Then adjust the size of the repeat squares (these may not correspond to the size of the stencil block) to make an even grid.

Fold the fabric in half widthways and mark the centre line in tacking stitches. Mark the midpoint of this line.

Measuring carefully and scaling up the graph, divide the fabric into parallel lines, working out from the centre.

Return to the midpoint of the fabric and work outwards along the centre line, measuring off and marking the width of the squares.

Find the midpoint of the two outer lines and mark them off in the same way.

Complete the grid by joining these points with tacking stitches.

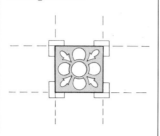

Painting the stencil

To paint the stencil, lay the block on the right side of fabric and attach with masking tape.

Pour fabric paint into an old saucer and apply with either a stiff stencil brush or a firm paintbrush.

Always start with a small amount of paint on the brush and build up colour gradually by dabbing lightly with the bristle tips on the exposed area of the fabric.

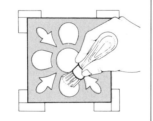

For multicoloured motifs, apply the palest shades first, then continue through to the darker tones, allowing ample drying time between each coat.

FABRIC MARKER PENS

One very simple way of decorating fabric with stripes, geometric or abstract designs, stencils or even free-hand drawing is to use felt tip pens containing a solution of fabric dye. Follow the painting methods previously described and, if the felt tip becomes dry, apply fabric ink directly on to the tip.

PAINTING FINE FABRICS

When decorating delicate fabrics, such as silk, with fabric paints, there is a tendency for the colours to 'bleed', giving the design a smudged look. To prevent this, paint the fabric with an anti-diffusing agent first, completely covering its surface. When this has dried, fine lines and details can be painted without smudging.

Allow the design to dry and fix the colours according to the manufacturer's instructions, then remove the anti-diffusing agent by rubbing gently under cold water.

Another way of preventing colours running when painting fine fabrics is to outline the design in a resist called 'gutta', which is available in a limited range of colours plus neutral. Make sure there are no gaps in your gutta outline through which the paint can escape.

When the gutta is dry the design can be filled in. Colour should be applied sparingly with a soft paintbrush, working out from the centre.

When outlining or painting an intricate design on fine fabric without the aid of a stencil, trace the design on to the fabric in pencil first. (See PRICKING AND POUNCING for an alternative method of transferring a design.) If the fabric has been pinned to softboard, use a backing sheet of blotting paper to absorb any excess paint.

PRICKING AND POUNCING

This method of transferring a design was used in the 16th century when embroidering as a pastime became increasingly popular.

Choose a colour of powdered tailor's chalk (the 'pounce') that will show on the fabric. Lay a sheet of tracing paper over the design and trace it. Next machine stitch around the outline of the design to make small, even perforations in the tracing paper or prick holes by hand. The holes should be close enough together so that the details of the design will show through when the design is transferred.

Pin the pricked design on to the framed fabric. Dip a pad of cloth into the powdered chalk and dab it over the tracing, forcing chalk through the holes on to the fabric beneath. Remove the tracing carefully. Lightly pencil in the outline.

INDEX

ACKNOWLEDGMENTS

The publisher thanks the following photographers and organizations for their kind permission to reproduce the photographs in this book:

Ambiente/Bent Weber **54–55**; reproduced by permission of The American Museum in Britain, Bath **40**; Arcaid (Richard Bryant) **16–17** (Lucinda Lambton) **152**; Roland Beaufre/Top, Paris (at the home of F.X. Lalanne) **21**; Michael Boys **24**; Bridgeman Art Library/Szepmuveszeti Museum, Budapest **36**; Guy Bouchet **71**, **75** *below*, **97**, **124–5**; Camera Press **48–49**, **82**, **94–95**, **108**, **156–7**, **176–7**; reproduced courtesy Cameron books **38–9**; 100 Idées (Chabaneix/Garçon) **168–9** (Duffas/Schoumacher) **93**; Gilles de Chabaneix **15**, **45**, **46–7**, **60**, **72–3**, **75** *above*, **117**, **126–7**, **153**, **155**, **174–5**, **185** (designer A. Comar) **74**; Collier Campbell **170–171**; **37** Susan Collier/CO; Jacques Dirand from French Style by Stafford Cliff **14**, **129**, **135**, **163**; Futon Company **136–7**; Jean Pierre Godeaut (designer Jacques Grange) **23**; Good Housekeeping (Jan Baldwin) **86–7** (David Montgomery) **18–19**; Susan Griggs Agency/Michael Boys **11**, **102–3**, **180–181**; Habitat **131**, **183**; François Halard **56**, **65**, **70**; Pascal Hinous/Top, Paris (designer Frederic Mechiche) **13** (designer Jacques Grange) **84–5** (designer D. Kiener) **122–3** (designer J.P. Hagnauer) **154–5**; Ken Kirkwood from English Style by Stafford Cliff **28**, **81** *right*, **90**, **105**, **187**; Ralph Lauren Home Collection **120**, **178–9**; Maison Française (Arcadia) **161** (Christian Gervais) **121** (Philippe Leroy) **68–9**, **114**; Maison Marie Claire (Eriaud/Comte) **17** (Chabaneix/Rozenstroch) **28–29** (Bouchet/Bayce) **52** (Eriaud/Comte) **61** (Rozès/C. Hirsch-Marie) **78–9** (Perrotte/Berthier) **118** (Berthier/McLean) **133** (Pataut/Bayle) **142–3**; Marie Claire (Godeaut/Pompon Bailhache) **113** (Halard/Pompon Bailhache) **28**; Bill McLaughlin **50**; Derry Moore **25**, **63**, **118–9**, **146–7**, **167**; Eric Morin (designer Jacques Grange) **20**; Michel Nahmias **52–3**; National Trust Photographic Library/John Bethell **33**; Osborne & Little **99**; Jacques Primois **151**; designer Andrée Putnam **88–9**; Bent Rej **132**; Ianthe Ruthven (designer Denis Severs) **38–9**; Mary Ryde from 'Victorians at Home' Susan Lasdun, Weidenfeld & Nicolson, 1981 **42**; Souleiado **144–5**, **158–9**, **193**, Joe Standart, Millennium **189**; Jessica Strang (stencils by Lyn Le Grice) **66**; John Vaughan (Amsterdam) **26–7**, **58–9**, **83** *above*, **107**; John Vaughan (San Francisco), (designer Michael Taylor) **140–141**; Deidi von Schaewen **43**, **49**, **91**, **114–5**, **116**; Elizabeth Whiting & Associates (Michael Dunne) **12–13**, **22**, **81** *left*, **173**; The World of Interiors (James Mortimer) **67**, **168** (John Vaughan) **9** (John Vere Brown) **34–5**

The following photographs were taken especially for **Conran Octopus**:

Simon Brown (artist/sculpture Elyane de la Rochette) **10** (architect Ian Hutchinson) **57**; Ken Kirkwood **30–31**; Clive Streeter **92**, **100–101**, **110–111**, **138–139**, **148–149**, **164–165**, **190–191**